The Theory of the

Governance of Jurist

(Wilayat al-Faqih)

Mahdi Hadavi Tehrani

Translated by
Hossein Pirnajmuddin

Published by
Islamic Centre of England
200

The Theory of the Governance of Jurist (Wilayat al-Faqih)

First published in the UK by Islamic Centre of England
140 Maida Vale, London W9 1QB, UK
Tel: 020-7604 5500
Fax: 020-7604 4898
Email: icel@ic-el.org
Homepage: www.ic-el.org
ISBN: 1-904934-02-1

Contents

Preface

Undoubtedly, the theory of 'the governance/guardianship of the jurist/jurisconsult' (*wilayat al-faqih* in Arabic, *wilayat-i faqih* in Persian) has been one of the most controversial political debates in Iran and the world for the last two decades. It is probably the most important theoretical issue in the domain of contemporary political thought. The formation of a government based on this theory by Imam Khomeini (*qudissa sirruh*), the great reviver of Islam in our age, has raised many questions about it.

This book is a brief survey of the speculative underpinnings of the idea of Islamic government and its theological and legal premises. In chapter I, 'Premises', I have tried to answer the most fundamental theological questions about religious government in general and Islamic government in particular. Chapter II, '*Wilayat al-Faqih*' (governance of the jurist), addresses the historical background, rational and 'transmitted' arguments as well as the limits and conditions of 'the governance of the jurist' answering the most significant, and probably the most recent, demurs about it.

May God and the Lord of the Age accept this humble effort.

Praise be to Allah.
Mahdi Hadavi Tehrani (Professor in Islamic Law)
1997

Chapter I - Premises

- Introduction
- What is religion?
- The perfect religion
- The paradox of immutable religion and the changing world
- The immutable and mutable elements of religion
- Theory of systematic thought in Islam
- Religion and science
- *Faqih's* (the jurist's) management, scientific management
- Islamic political system at a glance

Introduction

When we come up with a question about religion and seek the answer, first we have to clarify our position. Do we seek the answer from the viewpoint of a religious person or not? This raises other questions. What is religion? To what domain of religious teachings does our question pertain? What is the way to find the answer to it?

Questions about government are no exception to this general rule; hence a clear idea of the aforesaid questions is necessary before addressing them. Furthermore, there are other questions to answer too. How can a constant, immutable religion meet the requirements of an ever-changing world? Where do the immutable and mutable components stand in religion? How do they relate? We will touch on all these questions as an introduction to the discussion of *wilayat al-faqih*; that is, the manifestation of 'government and religion' in the age of occultation (*ghayba*).

What is religion?

There are numerous interpretations and views of 'religion' (*din*).[1] Some regard any belief in the occult, including superstitions and illusions, as religion. They view religion only from the sociological standpoint, measuring religious thought against the empirical yardstick. As such, no distinction is made between superstitions and cogent beliefs.

From a divine outlook, however, religion is a set of beliefs, tenets and guidelines spelled out by God through His

---

[1] See John Hick, *Philosophy of Religion*, Englewood Cliffs, 1989.

prophets for guiding man. In this reading, 'religion' has an essential, ideal truth and an objective reality, which is sometimes correctly understood and sometimes misunderstood. Thus, in this view the false beliefs that the followers of a religion come to hold or the erroneous interpretations of religious truths are not regarded as part of that religion.

The perfect religion

If we view religions from such a perspective, we will see that each religion has come to guide people at a particular time hence the advent of different religions with each new one adding some new elements to its predecessor.

Moreover, false beliefs and distortions would gradually begin to creep into a religion which the new religion would set about refuting and rectifying. Thus each religion both complemented and rectified its predecessor; this complementation and rectification went on continuously until the advent of the most perfect religion. This religion is the sublime Islam, the last religion with the Koran as its book. While enjoying ultimate perfection and embracing all that man needs for his salvation till the end of time, it has remained free of all distortions and changes.

The paradox of immutable religion and the changing world

How could possibly there exist a religion containing all that man needs for salvation eternally? How could a religion eternally guide man who is so much susceptible to change, vicissitude and evolution?

Faced with this question, some have totally waived such a

claim and have ignobly accepted that the secret of being the final religion lies in that man can dispense with Divine guidance as a result of the perfectibility of his reason!

If this was true, however, man should have obtained his independence from religion and been able to achieve salvation by just relying on his reason a few centuries after the advent of Islam.

Contemporary history proves this to be absolutely false. Far from feeling religion to be unnecessary, after defying it in and after the Renaissance and going through many traumatic experiences, man now increasingly feels closer to and more then ever in need of it.

Another group addressing this question have adhered to the theory of perfectible and progressive religion claiming that simultaneous with man's growth the final religion also evolves and accommodates itself to new circumstances. This idea makes religion susceptible to change and denies the eternal, timeless nature of its teachings.

Others have heeded the above consequence and by differentiating between 'religion' and 'religious cognition' have attempted to solve the problem in a way as to avoid the aforementioned false outcome. They say the 'essence of religion' is immutable but 'religious cognition' is mutable and in keeping with human progression.

They have also taken note of the fact that something variable and subject to degeneration cannot be 'sacred'. Hence they hold that 'religion' (of Islam) is immutable and sacred but religious cognition is variable and profane. What man can attain, however, is 'religious cognition' and the actuality of 'religion' will forever remain unattainable. This unearthly religion will in no way affect the life of the earthly man and even does not conform to the definition of religion. For religion, as we said before, is a totality of teachings laid down by God and communicated through the prophets.

If we acknowledge what God has laid down and is recorded in religious texts as 'religion' (*din*) and nonetheless insist on the inevitable change and vacillation in religious cognition and perception, we will in reality make religion subject to mutation upholding the previous solution in a new garb. Consequently, we will come up with the problem of saying: such a religion cannot be sacred.

To solve this problem without being misled and be on the right path, not just on the 'path', we have to contemplate man's conditions to find out if indeed he is always changing and all his affairs are subject to alteration. Or is there an unchangeable and permanent core to this shell of change, one connecting man's past, present and future and makes him a present identity in the course of history endowing human culture and civilisation with meaning? Whereas man's faculty of intellect develops and his behaviour changes he enjoys constancy of nature and permanence of selfhood. The change in social relations, costume, life-style and tools will never change his nature and instincts.

The fundamental questions of man's life throughout his tempestuous history have always remained unchanged. His feelings and sensibilities have also defied change so that the poems of Homer and Ferdausi still move him.

Religion targets this immutable core of humankind. Thus religious doctrines are constant and unalterable and, having this characteristic, enjoy 'sanctity'.

The immutable and mutable elements of religion

From what was said it follows that the perfect religion contains all the eternal teachings involved in man's salvation. This is what reason allows, not deeming more than this as necessary for the perfection of religion.

Hence, if the last religion had confined itself to expressing the constant, ubiquitous and timeless elements without so much of hinting at the variable and contingent ones, from a rational viewpoint it would not have been deemed flawed at all.

But it has not been the case. The sublime Islam has not just expressed the eternal, universal elements but has also addressed the contingent and time-bound issues.

It follows that we believe that the Holy Prophet of Islam (Peace be upon him and his progeny) in addition to his prophetic mission and communicating the constant, universal teachings enjoyed *Imamat* and articulated and dealt with the contingent issues of his time. In other words, the Holy Prophet (Peace be upon him and his progeny) while delivering the immutable fundamentals, as the perfect Muslim, would also illustrate the variable components and contingencies arising at his time based on these immutable elements. As such he entered the arena of running the society and by forming the first Islamic government exemplified the ordering of the Islamic society in accordance with divine objectives.

Seen this way, it becomes manifest how *'wilai'* (pertaining to *wilayat al-faqih* or governance of jurist) commands (*hukm*)' are formed alongside 'divine commandments'. 'Divine commandments' are immutable and universal while 'commandments pertaining to *wilaya*' are the mutable and contingent decrees stemming from the permanent ones in particular circumstances. In fact the immutable decrees underlie the mutable ones; or, put another way, the contingent and mutable decrees are the outcome of the constant and universal ones in particular situations.

The relation between the immutable and mutable elements

The rich Islamic teachings are full of universal and contingent components that have been articulated from the beginning of the mission of the Holy Prophet (Peace be upon him and his progeny) to the major occultation (*al-ghaybat al-kubra*) of the last Imam, Lord of the Age, (May God hasten his advent).

An atomistic approach has been for most part followed in trying to answer the questions raised in this regard. In this approach no notice has been taken of the link either between the unchanging elements themselves or between these and the changing ones. All aspects of the religion (of Islam) are taken to be constant and unchangeable unless something proves to be otherwise which in that case it would be regarded as a '*wilai* command' without attempting to find the divine decree or decrees underpinning it.

This trend has culminated in the lack of a comprehensive and systematic perspective in Islamic debates and studies and the random juxtaposition of the structural components of the Islamic thought. Although this juxtaposition has ultimately brought about some kind of order, the logical interrelation of the components and their interdependence has never been probed.

Moreover, the status of the Holy Prophet (Peace be upon him and his progeny) and the Infallible Ones (*ma'sumin*) as *wali* (having *wilaya* (governance / guardianship)) has not been noted and all their statements have been treated as 'divine decrees'; if in some cases there have existed manifest signs of *wilaya*, it has simply been counted as a *wilai* decree without questioning its foundations.

Such an approach may be practical in a non-Islamic or a pre-modern Islamic state but in a modern Islamic state it will come up with many problems. That is why we see that by the advent of the Islamic government in Iran and the move towards running a contemporary society by Islamic standards the idea of the role of time and place in *ijtihad* (independent reasoning/interpretation) has increasingly come to the fore and is now posed as a basic question for *faqih*s (jurists) and Islamicists.

Where the role of time and place is most crucial is undoubtedly the domain of mutable decrees and judgements that are tied up with particular situations, times and places. This is not, however, the only domain in which these two elements (time and place) are of consequence. Furthermore, even in this area the way these elements operate and interact needs to be thought through and investigated.

Also, in the domain of the immutable elements, the link between the components in either spheres of individual and social matters as well as the relation between the components of each sphere with other spheres are yet to be scrutinised.

Such ambiguities have resulted in our not being able, on the one hand, to put forward coherent Islamic agendas in different areas such as economy, politics, education, etc. and, on the other, not to have a clear idea of the field of influence of time and place and the way they come to be influential.

Thus, it is essential to codify, in the light of a systematic perspective, the immutable elements in different spheres of man's life such as economy, politics, law, etc. and articulate their interaction. Moreover, we have to explicate the logical link between the immutable and mutable matters and distinguish between the field of action of the experts in religion and those in other sciences as well as the grounds for joint action and its manner.

We have called this systematic approach 'the theory of systematic thought in Islam' which will be briefly explained.[2]

The theory of systematic thought in Islam

The theory of systematic thought in Islam is a systematic

---

[2] What follows is the third edition of this theory. The first and second editions are already presented in, respectively, the introduction to the essay 'The general structure of the Islamic system of economics' and the essay 'The theory of systematic thought in Islam'. The fourth edition is forthcoming as 'The theological foundations of *ijtihad*'. See Mahdi Hadavi Tehrani, 'The general structure of the Islamic system of economics', *Proceedings of the Fifth Conference on Koranic Sciences and Concepts* (Persian), Qum, 1993 and Mahdi Hadavi Tehrani, 'Theory of systematic thought in Islam' (Nazariye-ye andishi-ye modavvan dar eslam) *Proceedings of the Conference on Surveying the Legal Foundations of Imam Khomeini's Thopught, the Role of Time and Place in Ijtihad*, 1995, vol.3.

approach in the study of religion and ultimately aims at answering the following fundamental questions:

1. How can a constant, immutable religion be in charge of a changing, protean world?

2. What can be expected of religion in different spheres of man's social life?

3. How are we to attain that which is to be taken from religion?

4. What is the logical link between science and religion?

5. In what areas and how can the experts in religion and sciences co-operate?

This theory consists of three parts:

1. Theological premises

2. The main body

3. Methodological results

1- The theological premises

The 'theory of systematic thought in Islam' is predicated on several premises, hinted at before, which are all our unambiguous, fundamental beliefs. These are:

a. Religion has delivered all that is necessary for man's salvation.

b. Islam is the final religion; that is, it incorporates all that man needs at all times in all places.

c. The essential function of religion is to deliver universal principles, laws and values (pertaining to all times and places).[3]

d. The Holy prophet (peace be upon him and his progeny) in addition to '*risala*' (mission, prophethood, messengership), which entailed communicating and exposing universal laws and decrees, also enjoyed '*Imamat*' that required considerations conditioned by different circumstances (pertaining to particular times and places) and as such he has also addressed the situational, contingent (related to time and place) elements.[4]

e. The universal and the contingent (situational) elements of Islam are often intertwined.

f. The universal elements have a systematic relationship with each other and with the contingent elements.

The first four items have already been partly explained. As a note on 'd' we should add that the Infallible Ones (Peace be upon them) undertook the communication of both the universal and the contingent components, enjoying the Holy prophet's succession in either of these stations. Hence, what is meant by the intertwining of the universal and the contingent elements in 'e' is the totality of *sunna*, the sayings and doings of the Holy Prophet (Peace be upon him and his progeny) and the Holy Imams (Peace be upon them).

Intersection of the universal and contingent (situational) elements- Although the notion of immutable and mutable constituents has a long history, perhaps dating back to early Islam, and some issues have been regarded as *wilai*

---

[3] It is called 'deriving the divine law'.

[4] Also called 'deriving *wilai* (of *wilaya*) laws'.

(pertaining to *wilayat al-faqih*) and related to particular circumstances, there has always been the impression that the variable constituents have been couched in an idiom independent of the constant elements so that there could be a demarcation between the arguments for immutable laws and those for the mutable decrees.

In this view the whole of the Koran and a good part of the *sunna* of the Infallible Ones (Peace be upon them) are counted as the unchanging components of the sacred religion of Islam and only a few cases are considered as mutable for which numerous proofs and examples are adduced.

The reality, however, is that *risala* (prophethood) and *Imamat* overlap and even though at times we only see the statement of the universal laws, in the majority of cases, or at least in a good number of them, it is not so but the immutable law has been articulated in regard with a particular situation so that it consists of both the universal and contingent decrees. This is to be found even in the Koran; that is, a universal, general issue has been stated with respect to a particular case and even at times the particulars of the case may have been incorporated.[5] Thus, each Koranic verse (*aya*) has an occasion of revelation (*al-sha'n al-nuzul*), that is, it has been revealed (sent down) at the most appropriate time to have the best impact and get the message across more clearly.

Therefore, we brush aside the minutiae of particular instances and in keeping with the rule of 'a general law or principle is not to be inferred from a particular instance' we look for a general, permanent, all-inclusive and, in fine,

---

[5] Such as the uses of *zakat* (alms tax) as viewed by some *faqih*s.

universal principle. We are well aware of the fact that unless we do so and avoid getting stuck in the particulars of individual instances, we will question the permanence of the Koran, the eternal miracle of the Holy prophet (Peace be upon him and his progeny), and entertain doubts about this clear doctrinal foundation and its general, perennial guidance.

However, we should not lose sight of the fact that it is possible for the particulars of an instance to have been incorporated in the Koranic (general) statement so that in order to arrive at the clear, constant source some of these particulars have to be taken into consideration. Viewed this way, we cannot simply divide the religious sources and texts into a majority evidencing immutable laws and a minority evidencing mutable laws and rules. But every text and statement should be investigated for possible variable and contingent elements. On the other hand, we should not gloss over some laws as simply mutable and have to seek the immutable law or laws underlying them.

For example, nowadays despite the dominant *fatwa* (legal opinion) of the *faqih*s to the effect that in manslaughter [6] blood-money (*diya*[7]) is on *'aqila*[8] (the mature and sane person), some hold that such a decree pertains to the time of tribal relations and now that such relations are no longer

---

[6] When the person causing murder has neither had malice aforethought nor any intention of doing something culminating in murder, his crime is said to be manslaughter, 'total inadvertence' (*khata-ye mahz*). For example, when someone aims at a bird but his shot kills a man.

[7] *Diya* is the money that should be paid as a recompense for manslaughter.

[8] By *aqila*, in the first place, is meant blood relations such as brother, uncle and their children.

extent there is no rationale for such decrees or judgements. In contrast to the dominant view which considers the decree under discussion as immutable, timeless and applicable everywhere, they insist on its changeability and its absolute dependence on the situation and context. They assume that by arriving at this legal decision they have solved the problem once and for all asserting that since the general rule is that everyone is responsible for his own crime it follows that in manslaughter payment of blood-money is on the perpetrator themselves.

They have not bothered to ask: if indeed this decree (payment of blood-money being on 'aqila in manslaughter) was a mutable and contingent one concerned with tribal relations, how come the sublime Islam has accepted it and endorsed such a tribal custom? Is it not the case that underlying this changeable decree there lie unchanging injunctions and principles necessitating the passing of such a legal judgement in that context? And do these immutable decrees and principles have no other application today except proving the payment of blood-money in manslaughter to be on the person involved themselves? Perhaps the payment of blood-money by the blood-relatives has been a kind of public insurance the modern from of which is the undertaking of this payment by an institution.

Of course all this is given as an example and the discussion of a legal judgement or ruling is not intended. What is to be emphasised is: (1) the immutable and mutable decrees or, more precisely, the universal and contingent elements of Islam are presented in an interwoven manner in religious texts, including the Koran and traditions, so that it is not easy to categories the texts into a majority evidencing immutable decrees and a minority evidencing mutable ones. Indeed, we have to have a tripartite division of the texts in which there are two minor categories, one only evidencing universal elements and the other evidencing only the contingent as well as a third major category containing the universal and contingent side by side or even intertwined. A closer look will again lead us to a binary division since the contingent is always predicated on the universal. Hence the religious sources and texts are to be divided in two categories: a minority indicative of the immutable, universal laws and decrees, and a majority indicative of a combination of the universal and the contingent components; (2) whenever a decree is called mutable and contingent the universal components occasioning its application in a particular situation have to be searched out; it is even possible that these universal elements also have a special application at present.

Here we are concerned with the relationship of the universal elements with each other and with the contingent components. The universal elements form a system in either of the private and public spheres of man's life. This system consists of constant, immutable and eternal components, what we can expect of 'religion' in that particular sphere. This aspect is sacred as it is the immutable core; it is also approachable and learnable and consists of the fundamental guidelines of the prophets and their indelible teachings.

At the same time the immutable elements have special applications and adaptations which are related to both the religion and time. These are also affected by the universal components.

2- The main body

The theory of the systematic thought in Islam with respect to
the aforesaid theological premises is postulated as the logical
conclusion to these premises. According to this theory Islam
has a set of universal, immutable teachings in each of the
private and public domains of man's life which comprise the
Islamic system in that domain. We call this set the 'system'.
For instance, 'the Islamic political system' is the set of
perennial blueprints that Islam posits in the realm of politics
independent of any particular time or place.

Alongside these universal components there are also
contingent constituents in each domain the totality of which
we call 'mechanism'. Thus, while in the sphere of politics
we only have one 'Islamic political system', in accordance
with time or place and geographical position, or, to put it
another way, in accordance with the 'context', including all
that is involved in politics, we have different mechanisms.
The Islamic politics at the time of the Holy Prophet (Peace
be upon him and his progeny) is one of these mechanisms
designed with respect to the climatic, cultural, social,
economical and political situation in Arabia in early Islam.

As such, what the sublime Islam has offered us in every area
of life, either private or public, is a harmonious, coherent,
constant and eternal whole which can set a model for
individual and social activities of man throughout history.
Alongside this invaluable treasure we have the adaptation
and application of this whole by the Holy Prophet (Peace be
upon him and his progeny) and the Infallible Ones (Peace be
upon them) at their time. This adaptation provides us with
instances of Islamic mechanisms in different areas according
to which the proper Islamic mechanism in keeping with a

particular context (time and place) can be designed.

The 'system' and 'mechanism' produce a set of regulations that we call 'laws'. As such the 'Islamic political laws' is a set of rules and guidelines engendered in line with the 'Islamic political system' and 'Islamic political mechanism'. Therefore, immutable laws also include mutable rules conditioned by particular circumstances.

It follows that in every domain of man's life we have three sets: system, mechanism and laws.

A- The system

Every worldview has its own interpretation of man, his relation with the world and the source of existence. This interpretation has diverse manifestations in different spheres of human life. Each manifestation is in fact the system presented by that worldview in a particular sphere. For instance, Islamic worldview in the field of politics has a manifestation that we call 'Islamic political system'. Thus, 'system' is the logical and inevitable culmination of a worldview in a domain, individual or social, of human life. In other words, the propositions and premises in a 'system' are the extensions of those of the relevant worldview and since the worldview is constant and immutable it follows that the components of the system are also invariable and independent of time and place. Therefore, a system is a totality of propositions propounded by a worldview in a particular sphere of man's social or individual life; these propositions have three characteristics: (1) they are universal and independent of time and place; (2) they are all related to a particular sphere such as politics; (3) they are descriptive.

The universality of the components of a system- The interpretation by a worldview, even a secular one, of man, his origin and end and the world is universal and independent of a particular time or place. Put another way, from the standpoint of an adherent of a worldview it is universal, even though it may indeed have gone astray.

Hence, the 'system', which is the manifestation of a worldview in a sphere of man's life, is also universal. The universality, then, from the perspective of a proponent of a worldview or system means the applicability and practicality of the propositions of that worldview or system at all times and everywhere.

The perfect religion also has an interpretation of the source of existence, its destination and man's place in all this, which is independent of time and place. This Islamic interpretation of existence and the world has a logical and inevitable outcome in each of human life's domains which forms the Islamic system in that domain.

The link between the elements of a system and its relevant domain- As mentioned before, the manifestation of a worldview in every area of man's life is the system presented by it hence all the elements of that system are relevant to that particular area. For example, the components of 'the Islamic political system' are all relevant to politics.

The declarative nature of a system's elements- The postulations of a worldview in a particular area are sometimes prescriptive and in 'shalt / shalt not' form and sometimes descriptive and in the 'is / is not' form. Therefore, we divide the postulations with regard to their form--not content-- in two categories: prescriptive and descriptive or imperative and declarative.

The declarative constituents of a system or 'mechanism' could be created (*takwwini*) and real or hypothetical and legislated (*tashri'i*). The imperative or mandatory constituents, appearing in 'laws', are all hypothetical though this hypothesis may have its foundation in a created reality. Thus, the elements of the system are stated in declarative and descriptive propositions whether their content be created and real or hypothetical and legislated.

The proposition '*faqih* has *wilaya* (governance/ guardianship)' is considered as an element in 'the Islamic political system' even though its content is a hypothesis as *wilaya* in this proposition is only a hypothesis.

The perfect system and the coherence of its components- A system is perfect only when it includes all the universal elements in a domain. The Islamic systems have this characteristic because they have their origin in the perfect religion. Put another way, the perfect religion presents perfect systems—systems possessing all the universal elements involved in man's prosperity in all spheres of his life. On the other hand, the elements of a system should all be in harmony with each other; there should not be the slightest discord and contradiction between them. Therefore, if we find discordant elements (say, in the Islamic political system), it will invalidate at least one of these elements, proving it to be incompatible with reality.

The link between the different systems of a worldview- Since the different systems of a worldview are all the logical culmination of that outlook in different domains of man's life, the premises of one conclusion and parts of one whole, they are interconnected and in accord with each other, their totality covering all aspects of human life. Hence, many of the components in different systems of a worldview are close to each other and are even different statements of the same reality. Moreover, these systems do not enjoy the same status in 'the configuration of systems' and in different worldviews they have different ways of relating to each other. For instance, in 'the configuration of Islamic systems' if we regard the five basic systems (social, political, educative (*tarbiyyati*), judicial and economic), we will arrive at the following conclusions:

a- The Islamic social system is the end result of other systems (political, economic, judicial and educative).

b- The Islamic political system in its realisation intersects with economic, judicial and educative systems.

c- Ideally, the Islamic educative system has primacy over the other systems.

d- The Islamic system of economics is in practice inclusive of the political system; is ideally subordinate to the educative system; and its manifestation is in the outcomes of the system of laws.

By 'a' is meant that the Islamic social system is in fact the end result of the set of Islamic systems in practice. Item 'b' means that the Islamic political system in practice overlaps with economic, judicial and educative systems and the structuring of each of them is in reality an institution of this system.[9]

Item 'c' takes note of the fact that the main objective of the mission of the prophets in general and the Holy Prophet of

---

[9] We will explain the terms 'system' and 'institution' in the theory of systematic thought later.

Islam (Peace be upon him and his progeny) in particular is the spiritual training and edification of mankind. The educative system of Islam, then, from the viewpoint of objectives, has priority over all the other systems; the other systems are there to realise this one.

In item d considering the definition of laws in all domains from the perspective of the theory of systematic thought and the existence of economic, political and educative, etc. laws and the fact that laws are the objective manifestations of each system it follows that the Islamic system of laws in the area of practical results is prior to all the other systems.

The last item refers to the fact that the Islamic system of economics, with all its importance in practice, is part of the political system in the area of objectives, subordinate to educative system and in practical results subject to the Islamic system of laws.

Although it is possible to find some of these issues in other worldviews too, their configuration is heterogeneous; that is, not only systems in different worldviews vary, the items in a configuration of systems are also discordant. For example, in materialist schools of thought, especially in communism, the economic system has priority over other systems in objectives so much so that even the educative system is dominated by the economic one.

Of course, it is impossible to give a clear picture of these issues in this brief introduction and what followed was meant to provide some sort of background for the next discussions.

The constituents of a system- A system consists of two main

constituents: (1) doctrine; (2) universal institutions. Doctrine
itself consists of two parts: (1) premises; (2) objectives.

The premises of doctrine in a system- The general principles
accepted as indisputable in a doctrine in a particular area on
which other components hinge are regarded as the premises
of that doctrine in a system. For instance, the following are
the premises of economic doctrine of Islam: (1) wealth and
value; (2) ownership; (3) economic freedom; (4)
distribution.

In the field of politics, some of the premises of the political
doctrine of Islam are: (1) the strong link between religion
and politics; (2) the attribution of absolute rule to God; (3)
the ownership of natural riches (resources) by the Holy
Prophet (Peace be upon him and his progeny) and the
Infallible Ones (Peace be upon them); (4) *wilayat al-faqih* in
the age of the occultation of the last Imam; (5) the
predication of laws on Islamic decrees; (6) the unity of the
Islamic *umma*; (7) the unity of the Islamic state; (8) the
universality of the Islamic state; (9) freedom of expression;
(10) respect for human emotions and instincts.[10]

All these matters are timeless and applicable everywhere
(universal) and are accepted by the sublime Islam as general
principles on which to found the other components of the
system in different areas.

The doctrinal premises in a system are sometimes
hypothetical (subjective considerations) such as wealth and

---

[10] For further discussion see Hassan Ali Karbalaian and Muhammad Riza
Kashifi, *Fihrest-e Sakhtar-e Mantiqi-ye Andishi-ye Siyasi dar Eslam* (*A
Survey of the Logical Structure of Thought in Islam*), ed. Mahdi Hadavi.

value, ownership and economic freedom in the Islamic economic doctrinal premises, *wilayat al-faqih* in the era of the occultation, freedom of expression and opinion in the foundations of the Islamic political doctrine, and sometimes created and real such as the attribution of absolute rule to the Almighty God in the Islamic political doctrine.

It has been already mentioned that although the components of the system are cast in a descriptive idiom, they may be hypothetical or real and created.

The doctrinal objectives in a system- The doctrinal objectives in a system are the ideals that are, mostly, real, and created. For instance, 'economic welfare' and 'distribution of wealth' are the constituents of the economic justice in the economic doctrine of Islam, the 'economic justice' itself being one of the ideals of this doctrine. The economic power of the Islamic state is also one of the ideals of this doctrine.

Similarly, issues such as 'creating the right environment for the growth of moral virtues and piety', 'the political authority of the Islamic state', 'internal and international security', 'justice in all areas', 'expansion and propagation of Islam' could be regarded as the objectives of the political doctrine of Islam.[11]

The ideals of each system, like the other components, are universal, descriptive and relevant to its context (economy, politics, etc.).

---

[11] *Ibid.*

Universal institutions- As mentioned before, a system consists of a doctrine and a set of universal institutions. Doctrine comprises objectives and premises, and 'universal institutions' refers to a set of institutions the interdependent functioning of which, in accordance with the doctrinal premises, realises the doctrinal ideals.

The 'universal institutions', then, consist of a set of 'immutable institutions' having the following characteristics: universality: institutions are independent of particular circumstances; realisable: the establishment of these institutions and their systematic functioning realise the ideals; based on the premises and targeting the objectives: since the 'universal institutions' are there to materialise the ideals in accordance with the fundamentals of the system they should have their basis in the doctrinal premises and aim at the materialisation of the doctrinal ideals; organised according to immutable laws: each comprehensive worldview contains a set of immutable rules in each sphere of man's life, which form the fixed institutions on the one hand, determine their interrelationship on the other and consequently, systematise them.

With respect to these characteristics the 'fixed institution' could be defined as 'the embodiment of the doctrinal fundamentals and ideals irrespective of circumstances and systematised by immutable laws'.

For example, some of the fixed institutions pertaining only to the Islamic state – fixed state institutions -- in the totality of economic universal institutions are: (1) the institution of state and public properties; (2) the institution of taxes; (3) the institution for economic policy-making; (4) the institution for economic programming; (5) the institution for supervising economic activities.

These fixed institutions are on the one hand related to the premises and on the other to the objectives of the economic doctrine of Islam. An example is the 'institution of taxes' which is premised on 'private ownership' and targets the distribution of wealth and economic welfare, i.e., economic justice. Of course this institution in Islam consists of a number of subsidiary institutions such as *khums* (one fifth religious tax on income), *zakat* (annual alms tax), *jizya* (poll-tax on non-Muslims) with the relevant immutable decrees determining their form and their relation with other institutions. From this perspective, non-compulsory immutable decrees much the same as compulsory ones are involved in the formation and systematisation of the institutions. [12]

System, doctrine and universal institutions

The following diagram outlines the foregoing discussion:

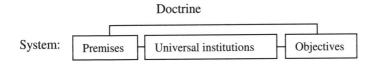

B- Mechanism

As stated before, the constant components in each domain

---

[12] As we will see the immutable commandments, mandatory or non-mandatory, apparently form the institutions and relate them in a systematic manner. But in reality the immutable commandments are formed on the basis of the universal institutions.

constitute the respective system in that domain which includes a doctrine and a set of universal institutions. These components are interwoven.

When a system is to operate in a situation it is inevitably affected by the particulars of that situation so that its institutions take on a special mould. This engenders a 'set of situational institutions' which we call 'mechanism'. These situational institutions have four characteristics: (1) situational: they are absolutely contingent on the circumstances; (2) practicable: they are realisable given the necessary conditions; (3) harmonious with the system: they are in fact a reflection of the fixed institutions in particular circumstances and are likewise in complete accordance with the system; (4) structured by mutable laws: there are a set of laws congruous with the circumstances affecting and structuring the respective situational institutions. These laws consist of compulsory and non-compulsory decrees. For instance, one of the private institutions (the fixed institutions which are not run by state, though state could also realise them) in the economic universal institutions of Islam is *qarz al-hasana* (loan without interest). Today that bank has become an indispensable part of the economic structure of our time this institution can function in the form of 'interest-free banking' whereas before the advent of bank this was not the case.

On the other hand it is possible to merge a number of the fixed institutions into a situational one or compartmentalise a universal institution into several variable ones as a way of streamlining the system. For example, in some circumstances the merger of 'the institution for supervising economic activities' with 'the institution for economic programming' may be desirable while in other circumstances the compartmentalisation of 'the institution for supervising economic activities' into the situational institution of 'supervising the public sector' and 'supervising the private sector' may be appropriate.

Finding the right mechanism in each situation depends on the one hand on a full knowledge of the system and on the other on the cognisance of the circumstances. Science can play a major role in the latter.

As such, the political mechanism of Islam in a particular situation, for instance, is designed with respect to the political system and the features of that situation while policy-making orchestrates its elements.

In some situations it is possible to have more than one postulated mechanism. In that case, the most efficient and accessible mechanism is to be preferred on a scientific basis.

Thus science plays a role both in the designing of mechanisms and determining preferability of some of them over others.

Accordingly, designing the appropriate political mechanism requires that, based on the political system and the data provided by political science, the situational institutions be set up and the mutable legal provisions determining and systematising them be established on the basis of the immutable laws pertaining the fixed institutions.

Indeed, what we see in the governance of the Holy Prophet (Peace be upon him and his progeny) is the political mechanism of Islam based on the conditions of the time which the Holy Prophet designed on the basis of the Islamic political system and the full understanding of the situation of Arabia at the time. Undoubtedly, the close study of this government in the light of the issues raised here can pave the way for designating the political mechanism in our era based on the Islamic political system.[13]

C- Laws

When a system with a certain mechanism is deployed in a society, in practice, it is in rules and legal provisions that it directly touches the individuals. We call the totality of these rules and legal provisions 'laws'.

Some of these 'laws' directly stem from the system itself and like it are independent of circumstances. We call these 'immutable laws'.

Another group of these laws originate in the mechanism and like it depend on a particular situation. These we call 'mutable laws'. Sometimes the immutable laws appear quite separately and sometimes in combination with the mutable laws in the form of a legal provision (judgement).

The doctrinal premises could be the source of the 'immutable laws', but it is not the case with the doctrinal objectives as they are ideals the realisation of which is only possible with the full deployment of the system. The set of universal institutions is the other source for the 'immutable laws', as the mechanism is the basis for the 'mutable laws'.

---

[13] We will shortly turn to the discussion of the extent and the manner of deploying the mechanisms used by the Imams (Peace be upon them).

The laws, whether immutable or mutable, are some obligatory and some conventional. The obligatory laws lead people to certain ways of living and bar them from certain others through compulsion, persuasion, prohibition, warning or permission. In contrast, the conventional laws authorise certain things and as such generate a set of rules.

The relation between system, mechanism and laws

Up to now we have tried to drive home the close relationship between the system, mechanism and laws. The diagram below epitomises what has followed:

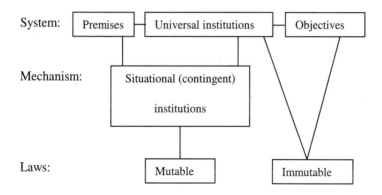

System, mechanism and laws in essence and in practice

What has been stated so far is the relationship between the worldview, system, mechanism and laws in essence. The manifestation of every worldview in each domain of man's life is its respective system in that domain. This system consists of a number of invariable and universal components and on the basis of some 'premises' propounds a set of fixed institutions in order to achieve certain ideals. These invariable institutions in particular circumstances create a mechanism that includes the set of contingent or situational institutions. The premises and fixed institutions are manifest in the 'immutable laws' while the influence of situational institutions is to be found in the 'mutable laws'.

In human doctrines such 'essential', 'intrinsic' realities remain the same in practice; i.e., at first a worldview is upheld, then there comes its embodiment in the form of a system in a particular aspect of man's existence followed by the respective mechanism, immutable and mutable laws.

It is not the case, however, with divine doctrines. A prophet or Imam may present the needed immutable or mutable laws without manifestly formulating the system or mechanism underlying them. For what is basically needed are the laws, the system and mechanism are required to realise them.

In other words, in human doctrines man arrives at a conception of the world and his position in it by dint of his thinking. Then interprets different aspects of his existence in that light and postulates a number of systems.

The more precise man's worldview, the higher are his chances of formulating more comprehensive systems. His means are reason and science by which he conceives the world and his status in it, then postulates the appropriate system in all aspects of his existence and legislates laws on the basis of these systems and mechanisms. He is not bound by any specific rule and constraint in this process and acts according to his reason and perception within the limits of which he interprets and legislates. If he regards man as absolutely free (liberalism), believes in the all-importance of man (individualism), sees this free man in quest of profit (utilitarianism) and conceives of the world as an arena of competition for gaining more and more pleasure, then he predicates each system in its respective domain on the liberty of individuals in that domain limited only by the liberty of others and sets as one, even the most important, of his ideals the attainment of as much pleasure as possible. For instance, his premises in the political system are the priority of individual opinions and the absolute freedom to take part in political activities, the objective: the acquirement of as much security and material welfare as possible. Likewise, in the universal institutions he gives primacy to free will as a means of achieving the objectives and finally establishes laws based on the system and mechanism which attend to the practical aspects.

In divine doctrines, however, though there is the same top-down configuration in essence, in practice it is otherwise. Namely, the omnipotent God has knowledge of man's position in existence, the ideals, premises, universal institutions in different spheres of man's life as well as how these institutions are to materialise in different circumstances. He has cognisance both of the immutable and mutable laws. But what is sent down for man through the prophets depends on the characteristics of each religion. If that religion is meant for a limited period of time, it meets the requirements of people in that period. If it is the last and final religion, however, succeeded by no other religion till the Day of Judgement, it has to meet the requirements of all times. The sublime Islam is such a religion.

Therefore, Islam, as the final and perfect religion contains all the universal and immutable blueprints as well as the contingent matters pertaining to the circumstances of the holy Prophet and Imams articulated by them. As such, some of the religious elements are comprehensive, universal and immutable whereas some are mutable and situational; also, in the Koran and *sunna* we find universal (descriptive or imperative) statements which in fact correspond to the constituents of different Islamic systems or the constant laws attendant upon them as well as contingent statements (descriptive or imperative) corresponding to the addressing of problems raised at the time of the Infallible Ones (Peace be upon them). The latter, the contingent issues related to the circumstances of the Infallible Ones (Peace be upon them), can also assist us in addressing our own issues. For it is possible to study the adaptation of a system's components by the Imams (Peace be upon them) in different situations as well as the mechanism employed by them, tease out all or some of the rules and principles underpinning this adaptation and obtain the discipline governing the relations between the components of the systems and mechanism. If we succeed in this we can consider our finding as part of an Islamic discipline, part of 'the science of Islamic politics' in the arena of politics, for instance.

In fine, what can be obtained from the Islamic sources consists of:

- Immutable elements (descriptive or mandatory) which comprise the Islamic systems, or the laws attendant upon them. In the light of what followed about the essence of religion and the final religion, these are undoubtedly extractable from the Islamic sources and will be a source of guidance for all the Muslims everywhere and at all times.

- The mutable elements (descriptive or mandatory) which

pertain to the circumstances of the Infallible Ones (Peace be upon them) and the corresponding mechanisms and laws. This is also certainly inferable from the Islamic laws, though it could be used only in circumstances identical with that of the Infallible Ones (Peace be upon them). In other words, in situations similar to that of the Imams (Peace be upon them) the use of the mechanisms put forward by them is mandatory because, as with religion, they have been cognisant of and free of mistakes in worldly affairs too.

• General methods for formulating Islamic mechanisms, which demonstrate the adaptation of the systems in different conditions. The extraction of these from the Islamic sources is possible and is what we mentioned before as part of an 'Islamic discipline' in different areas. If obtained, using these and compliance with their rules would be necessary.

3- Methodological result

In the light of our discussions it follows that we have to discover and resort to different systems, mechanisms related to the time of the Imams (peace be upon them) and probably part of the Islamic disciplines from the Islamic sources, the book (Koran) and the *sunna*. Furthermore, we have to search out the Islamic mechanisms fitting our time.

For this awesome task we need to find the right method for each case; that is, we need the appropriate methods both for what we seek in the book and the *sunna* and accessing the Islamic mechanisms.

A- Methods of discovering the systems

Since a 'system' relates to the worldview, laws and other systems, there are four ways of arriving at an Islamic system through the religious sources. First, top-down approach: by fully understanding the Islamic worldview and probing its manifestations in different facets of human life some components of Islamic systems could be discovered. The late Murtaza Muttahari has tried to search out the reflection of some of the fundamental beliefs such as 'justice' in the field of economy via this method.[14] Second, the direct approach: in this method the Islamic sources --the Koran and the *sunna* -- are referred to in order to identify some components of different systems stated in them or deducible from them.[15] Third, the bottom-up approach: by studying the laws and recognising their immutable elements we can find some components of the system underlying them. The late Sayyid Muhammad Baqir Sadr in his monumental *Eqtisaduna* (our economy) has tried to derive some of the constituents of the Islamic system of economics via this method.[16] Fourth, system – to – system approach: in this procedure we try to derive the components of a system (ex., economic system) from the components of another system (ex., political system). Of course this method is practicable only when we have already derived one of the systems through other methods.

---

[14] This is to be found in an unpublished book on economy.

[15] I have used this procedure in 'The general structure of the Islamic system of economics in the Koran' (Persian), *Proceedings of the Fifth Conference on the Disciplines and the Concepts of the Holy Koran*, Qum, 1992.

[16] Sayyid Muhammad Baqir Sadr, *Eqtisaduna fi Ma'alim al-Ra'isiya*, Beirut, 1982.

Only when all the aforesaid approaches have been tried it could be claimed that all the elements of an Islamic system have been derived. For though in essence each of these approaches would be adequate for discovering all the components of a system, in practice the limited nature of our knowledge may hinder us from deriving some of the elements through a certain approach and impel us to recourse to other approaches.

Naturally, if we come up with anything contradictory, it will prove some of our assumptions and conclusions to be wrong and will necessitate revision.

It should be noted that we have to reach a firm, accepted argument (*hujja*), to use a term in legal theory, in all these approaches. As such, we can say that in deriving the Islamic system and the laws attendant upon them we recourse to the juristic (*fiqhi*) methodology which, to be more precise, is 'the traditional jurisprudence and *ijtihad* as practised by the author of *Jawahir*'.[17]

It is obvious that the derivation of the component parts of the system is in line with and similar to the derivation of the

---

[17] Imam Khomeini in Manshur-e Ruhaniyyat (Charter of the Clergy) says:
As regards the method of religious education and research in the seminaries, I believe in the traditional fiqh (jurisprudence) and ijtihad (independent interpretation) as practiced by the author of Jawahir [Jawahir al-Ahkam by Shaykh Muhammad Hassan Najafi] and do not endorse anything else. That is the correct method of ijtihad.
These statements indicate that in Imam Khomeini's view 'the traditional fiqh and ijtihad as practiced by the author of Jawahir' is a method, an approach for gaining knowledge about Islam rather than a particular substance. See Mahdi Hadavi, 'Governmental fiqh and government based on fiqh' in Risalat (Persian daily) (1994), special issue on the fifth anniversary of the demise of Imam Khomeini.

laws attendant upon them. Hence it is enough to have available the methods of deriving the system to be able to deduce the immutable laws and vice versa.

B- The method of deriving the mechanisms used by the Infallible Ones

The mechanisms dealing with the circumstances of the Imams (Peace be upon them) include the contingent matters stated by them. To identify these matters we have to refer to the Islamic sources, the Koran and the *sunna*, and the historical writings of the time of the Imams (Peace be upon them) and make deductions via the juristic method of 'traditional *fiqh* and *ijtihad* as practised in *Jawahir*'. Thus, of the aforementioned methods two are to be used here: the direct approach: finding the variable elements related to the circumstances of the Infallible Ones (Peace be upon them) by referring to the Islamic sources and the historical writings of the time; the bottom-up approach: referring to the laws and identifying their variable elements in order to derive the whole or part of the mechanism underlying it.

C- The method of deriving some of the Islamic disciplines (sciences)

As mentioned before, it is possible to arrive at some of the Islamic disciplines, the methods of adapting the components of different systems to different circumstances. But as to date this area has not been put to the test of experience, there are not any reliable methods available. Though at times there emerge some hopeful signs of accessing them.

D- The sources for and the method of deriving the mechanisms

Discovering the mechanism compatible with a particular

situation has as its prerequisite the deriving of the Islamic system pertaining to that area. The next step is to identify the parameters affecting the adaptation of the universal institutions paying attention to the condition of people in that area. For instance, for designing the political mechanism applicable to Iran in our era the following steps are to be taken: (1) deriving the Islamic political system via the aforementioned approaches; (2) recognising the political situation of Iran and the world using the criteria in the political science; (3) identifying the parameters in the political situation of Iran and the world affecting the Islamic political system; (4) outlining the political mechanism with regard to the forgoing stages.

The contingent laws can easily be obtained after arriving at the right mechanism.

Religion and science

In the light of the theory of systematic thought in Islam we conclude that the main function of religion is to communicate the immutable essentials which are deducible from the religious sources via juristic (*fiqhi*) methodology. As to the mutable and contingent elements, however, they are as much tied up with circumstances as with the invariable religious elements.

Understanding the factors involved in a situation and the impact of each of them in particular areas is what human sciences are concerned with. Political science studies political relations and behaviour and the factors producing them as well as the effect each of these factors has on the political situation of a society. Thus, just as we need to derive the Islamic political system for discovering Islamic political mechanisms we also need political science that depicts the situation for us. This necessitates the collaboration of the experts in Islamic law (*mujtahid*s) and those in different sciences.[18]

The faqih's (the jurist's) management, scientific management

What followed was a very general outline of the position of religion in man's life. As mentioned, religion aims at putting human life on the way to perfection, true prosperity and happiness by presenting some universal principles and institutions. 'Management' from the Islamic standpoint, then, is the organisation of all the potentials of a society around the realisation of the high Islamic ideals. This also requires, in addition to the divine guidance, the contingent human sciences and the fruits of human reason. These sciences, the results of experience and ratiocination, enable man to understand different situations and the parameters of different phenomena. This ability, however, can prove beneficial and valuable only when it is subservient to religion. The *faqih*'s management, or, to put it more precisely, 'religious management' then, does not negate 'science' at all; far from running contrary to 'scientific management', it emphasises its sensible, comprehensive application.

On the other hand, sometimes there emerges the false assumption that 'the *faqih*'s management or administration' has little, if anything, in common with science and rationality and is in sharp contrast to 'scientific

---

[18] For further discussion see Mahdi Hadavi, 'Human needs and the eternality of religion' in *Majalli-ye Ma'arif* (Persian), 12 (1994).

management'. Sometimes this 'contrast' is emphasised to the point of intimating that 'running the society on the basis of religious values' via 'scientific methods' is self-contradictory. The implication of this assumption is that either it is completely impossible to run a society on the basis of divine values or the claim of experimental science being free from value judgement is to be seriously doubted. Many of those who accept the existence of this 'contradiction' are reluctant either to question the possibility of government in line with religious ideals[19] or refute the claim of science being free from value judgement.[20]

Sometimes they take this 'contrast' to arise from '*faqih*'s management/administration' and 'scientific management' being of different categories dealing with different subject matters. This is in some cases correct though it does not mean that religious management and governance is incongruous with science but indicates the necessity of revising and reinterpreting the findings of religious studies and experimental sciences.

At times, some contingent, variable phenomena in the domain of religion are counted as universal which is inconsistent with today's realities. Similarly, sometimes issues involving value judgement, hence outside the jurisdiction of science, are raised or unsubstantial claims of universality for branches of knowledge are made which are out of keeping with religious concepts.

---

[19] Of course some explicitly or implicitly do so!

[20] They would never admit the fact that branches of knowledge are subjective in degrees because it would undermine their claims of being scientific.

What is desired, then, is a full understanding of religion and the bounds of religious issues and debates as well as the way to adapt religion to every day realities. Of course science also has to confine itself to its own sphere and distinguish between objective realities and concepts dealing with values.

Islamic political system at a glance

The 'theory of systematic thought' postulates that Islam contains a set of immutable, eternal elements, independent of time and place, which are harmonious and form what we call a 'system'. 'Politics' has always been and is one of the most important aspects of man's life. Islam has also a coherent, comprehensive political system with national and international dimensions. This system consists of the doctrine and the set of universal institutions.

Although the 'Islamic political system' is in practice inclusive of all the other systems such as economic, judicial and educative but in theory it can be delineated in isolation.

Chapter II – Wilayat al-Faqih

- *Wilayat al-faqih*, conceptual analysis
- The importance of *wilayat al-faqih* in the Islamic political system
- The historical background
- Governance (*wilaya*) of the Infallible Ones, governance of *faqih*
- Proofs of *wilayat al-faqih*
- *Wilayat al-faqih* and people
- Governance of *faqih* or deputyship (*wikala*) of *faqih*
- Qualifications of *wali al-faqih*
- The limits of *wilayat al-faqih*
- Absolute *wilaya* of the *faqih* and totalitarian rule
- The constitution and absolute *wilaya* of *faqih*
- The concept of country and territory in Islam
- *Wilaya* and *marja'iyya* (religious authority)
- Dissociation of *marja'iyya* from leadership
- Multiplicity in leadership, multiplicity in *marja'iyya*
- The limits of following (*taqlid*) *marja*'s other than the leader
- Conclusion

Wilayat al-faqih: conceptual analysis

In Arabic 'wilaya' is derived from the root 'wali' which, in the words of the renowned Arabic lexicographers, is a single lexeme with a single meaning: nearness, affinity.[1]

There are three meanings recorded for the word 'wali' in Arabic: (1) friend; (2) devoted; (3) supporter. In addition to these[2], two other meanings have been mentioned for 'wilaya': (1) sovereignty and dominance; (2) leadership and governance.[3]

In Persian 'wali' has numerous meanings such as friend, supporter, owner, protector, deputy and custodian; also, 'wilaya' means: to rule, to govern.[4]

'Wilayat' in wilayat al-faqih means governance and administration. Some have taken this meaning to have the implications of 'mastership', 'lordship' and 'sovereignty' which indicate the authority of 'wali' (the bearer of wilaya) over 'mawla 'alayh' (one who is subject to wilaya).[5] Wilaya, however, means supervision and discharge of the affairs of 'mawla 'alayh' (as the saying has it: 'the leader of a people

---

[1] See *Maqa'is al-Lugha*, vol. 6, p.141; *Al-Qamus al-Muhit*, p. 1732; *Al-Misbah al-Munir*, vol. 2, p. 396; *Al-Sahah*, vol. 6, p. 2528; *Taj al-Arus*, vol. 10, p. 398.

[2] Some researchers have rejected the meanings of 'friendship' or 'support' for *wilaya* taking it to mean only 'sovereignty' or 'leadership'. See Muntaziri, *Dirasat fi Wilayat al-faqih wa Fiqh al-Dawlat al-Eslamiya*, vol. 1, p. 55.

[3] See *Al-Qamus al-Munir*, p. 1732; *Taj al-Arus*, vol. 1, p. 398; *Al-Misbah al-Munir*, vol. 2, p. 396.

[4] See Muhammad Mu'in, *Farhang-i Farsi*, vol. 4, pp. 5054 and 5058.

[5] See Mahdi Ha'iri Yazdi, *Hikmat va Hukumat*, pp. 76 and 177.

is their servant'); it is doing '*mawla 'alayh*' a service not an imposition on him.

Moreover, *wilaya* is used in two cases in juristic (*fiqhi*) terminology: (1) when *mawla 'alayh* is not able to discharge their own affairs as with the deceased, fool, insane and minor: (2) when *mawla 'alayh* can take care of their own affairs but there are matters and responsibilities which require the undertaking and supervision, *wilaya*, of someone else.

Wilayat al-faqih refers to the latter case as the '*faqih*' (jurist/jurisconsult), who has *wilaya* over the community, undertakes the guardianship of everyone including other *faqihs* and even himself. This is not due to the fault of 'society as society' as emphasised by some, comparing *wilayat al-faqih* with *wilaya* (custody/guardianship) over the deceased or *qussar* (the incapable: the insane, the fool, the absent and the minor) but due to the fact that every society needs someone to be in charge of its affairs.[6] Imam Ali (Peace be upon him) says: 'Every people needs a leader, be it righteous or corrupt'.[7] This is a social necessity. Wherever a society or group is formed there emerge certain communal issues and responsibilities which need to be undertaken by a leader or administrator. Of course Islam requires this leader or manager to have many qualifications the most important of which is having achieved *fiqaha* (the station of *faqih*), hence *wilayat al-faqih*.

As such, the *faqih* has *wilaya*, guardianship or governance,

---

[6] *Ibid.,* p. 177.
[7] Subhi Salih, *Nahj-ul-Balagha*, Khutba: 40, p. 82.

over society as a director or manager who impels it towards Islamic ideals; in fact, *wilaya* is the manifestation of religious management discussed before.

The importance of *wilayat al-faqih* in the Islamic political system

Probing 'the Islamic political system' and identifying its political doctrine we find one of the fundamentals of this doctrine to be '*wilayat al-faqih* in the absence or the occultation (*ghayba*) of the Holy Imams (Peace be upon them). As, in like manner, the 'affirmation of *wilaya* by God, sovereignty in the world of creation and divine legislation, or '*wilaya* of the 'Infallible Ones (Peace be upon them) from the Last Prophet (Peace be upon him and his progeny) to the Last Successor (*wasi*)' is one of the premises of political doctrine of Islam.

Accordingly, '*wilayat al-faqih*' is a cornerstone and a universal component of 'the political system of Islam' irrespective of the manner of realisation of the system and variation in the political mechanisms; only those forms of government or mechanisms are acceptable in Islam in which the status of the *faqih* in the era of occultation (*ghayba*) as the leader and the holder of the foremost position in the Muslim community is guaranteed.

The historical background

Some hold that the idea of '*wilayat al-faqih*' in the sense of a *mujtahid* (one who has achieved *ijtihid*) being in charge of the Islamic community is something novel in the history of Islamic thought and dates back to less than two centuries ago. They claim that none of the Shiite or Sunnite *faqih*s has postulated that the *faqih* besides the authority of issuing *fatwas*, in the capacity of one who is an authority in *fiqh* (jurisprudence), is entitled to the governance or leadership of one or all the Islamic countries or all the countries of the world and it was Mulla Ahmad Naraqi, alias Fazil Kashani, a contemporary of Fatih 'Ali Shah of Qajar in Iran, who for the first time put forward this idea less than two centuries ago. What is more, the reason for raising this issue by Naraqi is said to have been endorsing the then king![8]

Of course if Naraqi had wanted to vindicate the king, it would have served his purpose better to resort, like some preceding *ulama*, to traditions such as 'sultan is Shadow of God'[9] and apply them to the king whereby declaring obedience of him as divine and religious obligation. As it is, he has declared sovereignty and leadership to be the right of the *faqih*, a title which could never be applicable to the king.[10]

---

[8] See Ha'iri Yazdi, *Hikmat va Hukumat*, p. 178.

[9] See Majlisi, *Bahar al-Anwar*, vol. 72, p. 354 (Kitab al-Ashr, bab: Ahwal al-Muluk wa al-Ulama, hadith: 69). Of course in Imam Khomeini's interpretation these traditions refer to the Holy Imams or the *faqih*.

[10] It should be noted that there are two interpretations of traditions such as these. First, the person who rules and has dominance and sovereignty (*sulta* or sultanate) is Shadow of God whose obedience is obligatory. In this reading the characteristics of the ruler and the manner in which he has taken power has nothing to do with obedience of him being obligatory. No doubt, this interpretation has perfectly suited the rulers and kings and has justified the status qua. Second, the person who comes to have *sulta* [*sulta* and sultan having the same root] and be in charge of the administration of society must be the representative (Shadow) of God. That is, his character and manner of taking power must be verifiable by God and Divine law. In this interpretation, only the person who has the attributes of the ruler verified by Islam and has come to power in a manner sanctioned by it is to be obligatorily obeyed. The thesis of *wilayat al-faqih* takes the fully qualified *faqih* as having met these requirements.

If it is argued that he has first proved governance to be the right of the *faqih* and then has legitimised the rule of the king by endorsing it in the capacity of a *faqih*, the question raised will be; why doing it the hard way and not outright declare the king as the representative (Shadow) of God and obedience of him obligatory?

If it is suggested that maybe Naraqi having an eye to sovereignty has attributed this myth to Islam in order to satisfy his own desire, it is to be said that the life and personality of that great man give the lie to such calumnies and simplistic analyses; such claims accord with those who make them rather than that pious *faqih* and exemplar of morality (May God be pleased with him).

Apart from this, which is more of a tragic story than a scientific investigation, a look at the history of Islamic thought in this era shows that the idea of the running of society by *faqih*s of integrity in the era of occultation, authorised in Islam, has been taken as axiomatic in Shia thought, hence the discussions revolve around the consequences of this idea rather than its foundations.

Shaykh al-Mufid (d. 1022) was one of the great *faqih*s of Shia in the fourth and fifth centuries A.H. In his *Al-Muqna'i* discussing the religious obligation of enjoining the good (*al-amr bel-ma'ruf*) and prohibiting evil (*al-nahy an-al-munkar*) and explaining its respective stages, when he comes to the last stage, i.e. killing and injuring, he writes:

> The responsible person who is about to enjoin the good and prohibit evil has not the right to kill or injure unless he is authorised by the sultan or ruler of the time who has been appointed as the guardian and ruler of the people.

He continues:

> Enforcing religious sanctions and sentences is up to the Islamic
> rulers or religious (shar'i) arbitrators (hakims) who are
> appointed by God. They include the Holy Imams (Peace be
> upon them) and those appointed by them as ruler or arbitrator;
> the Holy Imams have entrusted the decision-making about this,
> where possible, to their Shia faqihs.[11]

In these remarks, which clearly betoken a fear of the rule of
tyrants, Shaykh al-Mufid (qudissa sirruh) puts forward the
idea of the appointment of the ruler by God recognising him
as the authority for deciding for or against killing or injuring
in enjoining the good and prohibiting evil. He then discusses
'enforcement of sentences' as a clear example of enjoining
the good and prohibiting evil and underscoring the
implementation of this important duty by the Islamic rulers
appointed by God enumerates them as: (1) the Holy Imams
(Peace be upon them) who are directly appointed by God as
leaders of the Islamic community and implementers of
divine laws and sanctions;[12] (2) the rulers designated by the
Infallible Ones (Peace be upon the them) as executives of
the Islamic community; (3) the Shia faqihs designated by the
Holy Imams (Peace be upon them) as heads of the Islamic
community and enforcers of the Islamic sharia (canonical
laws).

Thus, in addition to the governance and leadership of the
Holy Imams (Peace be upon them), axiomatic in Shia

---

[11] See Shaykh al-Mufid, Al-Muqna'i, p. 81.

[12] We will discuss some of the questions raised about wilaya, in the sense
of political leadership, of the Infallible Ones (Peace be upon them).

thought, Shaykh al-Mufid also refers to the specified representatives of the Holy Imams, individually appointed as political leaders such as Malik al-Ashtar at the time of Imam Ali (Peace be upon him) or the 'four representatives' in the era of the minor occultation (*al-ghaybat al-sughra*) of the Lord of our age (May God hasten his glad advent), and their general, unspecified representatives who are assigned leadership, that is, Shia *faqih*s.

Of course he takes into consideration the fact that it may not be possible for Shia *faqih*s to fulfil this divine responsibility, hence the stipulation 'where possible'. He proceeds to discuss cases where there is a greater degree of possibility of fulfilling part of this duty: 'If it is possible for a *faqih* to carry out the Islamic sentences about his children and retainers and avoid the threat of tyrannical, 'usurper' rulers, he must do so.[13]

These saddening remarks bespeak the repression of Shia thought in many Islamic historical periods and bear witness to the unambiguous and self-evident status of the idea of '*wilayat al-faqih*' in Shia thought and culture.

Shaykh al-Mufid then discusses another instance of the possibility of putting divine laws and obligations into practice:

> And this (the implementation of Islamic laws) is manifestly incumbent upon the person (the *faqih*) who has been appointed by the wielder of power to this task, or has been designated by him as the person in charge of a number of his subjects. Thus,

---

[13] See Shaykh Mufid, *Al-Muqna'i*, p. 810.

he must carry out Islamic sentences, implement religious injunctions, enjoin the good and prohibit evil and strive against the infidels (jihad).[14]

That is, if tyrannical sultans and usurper rulers designate a faqih a position in which he can implement Sharia without jeopardising himself, he must do so. Here Shaykh al-Mufid points out four issues: (1) carrying out Islamic sentences, which lies within the power of the Islamic ruler; (2) execution and enforcement of Islamic decrees including all religious injunctions and duties, accordingly the faqih has to do all he can to ensure the rule of Islam throughout and in all the affairs of the Islamic community; (3) enjoining the good and prohibiting evil, which at its higher levels is the concern of the Islamic ruler; (4) jihad and striving against infidels, which means defence against and also attacking them.[15]

Once again Shaykh al-Mufid focuses on this issue in an attempt to rule out any unfounded justifications and irrational interpretations:

It is incumbent upon the Shia faqihs, in case it is possible and they are safe from the persecution of the wicked, to congregate with their brethren in Friday prayer, prayers of the two festivals [Eid al-Fitr and Eid al-Azha], prayer for rain, moon-eclipse and sun-eclipse prayers. They must arbitrate justly and reconcile those who litigate each other but cannot adduce any evidence and implement all that Islam has assigned the judges. For the Holy Imams (Peace be upon them), according to their

[14] Ibid.

[15] One of the implications of this statement could be the possibility of declaration of limited jihad by the faqih, an issue which lies beyond the scope of our discussion though we will say a few words about it later.

> sound and valid traditions (*ahadiths*), verified by the experts,
> have entrusted the *faqih*s with the implementation, where
> possible, of these responsibilities.[16]

Here Shaykh al-Mufid underscores two important points: (1)
performing prayers such as Friday prayers, *Eid al-Fitr* and
Eid al-Azha prayers, prayer for rain; (2) arbitration and
adjudication. He considers both of these to be the
responsibility of the *faqih*s who are, he holds, designated on
the authority of sound traditions, by the Holy Imams (peace
be upon them). We will discuss these traditions about
wilayat al-faqih in some detail later. Here, however, note
should be taken of the crucial point that the sound traditions
about *Eid al-Fitr* and *Eid al-Azha* prayers, explicitly,[17] and
those about Friday prayer, implicitly,[18] make the stipulation
of the presence of 'the just Imam' (*Imam al-'adil*). Hence a
number of *faqih*s interpreting 'just Imam' or 'Imam of
integrity' (*Imam al-'adil*) as Infallible Imam (*Imam al-
ma'sum*) have not regarded these prayers to be obligatory in
the era of occultation. But Shaykh al-Mufid in fact
recognises the Shia *faqih*s as the referents of 'just Imam' by
taking the performing of the said prayers to be among their
duties. This accords with his earlier remark about '*jihad*
against the infidels' as one of the responsibilities of the
*faqih*s because it refers to limited *jihad* and the traditions
state that *jihad* is conditional on the presence of an Imam
obedience of whom is obligatory.[19] Some of the *faqih*s are of

---

[16] *Al-Muqna'i*, p. 811.

[17] Shaykh Hurr al-'Amili, *Wasai'l al-Shia'*, vol. 5, pp. 95-96 (Kitab al-
Salat, Abwab Salat al-'id, bab: 2, hadih: 1).

[18] *Ibid.*, pp. 12-13 (Kitab al-Salat, Abwab Salat al-Jum'i wa Adabuha,
bab: 5).

[19] *Ibid.*, vol. 11, pp. 32-35 (Kitab al-Jihad, Abwab Jihad al-'Adu, bab: 12).

the opinion that 'Imam' in these traditions refers only to Infallible Imams (peace be upon them), hence they have disallowed issuing the order of limited *jihad* by the *faqih*. In contrast, Shaykh al-Mufid believes that the Shia *faqih*, designated by the Holy Imams (peace be upon them) as guardian of the affairs in the era of occultation, is one of the referents of 'an Imam obedience of whom is obligatory, and thus can order limited *jihad*.

This great *faqih* of the Muslim world time and again underscores the principle of *wilayat al-faqih* and the governance by the *faqih*s of the Islamic community in the era of occultation, authorised by the Holy Imams (Peace be upon them). His invaluable remarks still scintillate after more than a millennium though some do not or do not want to notice them.

Discussing 'spoils' (*anfal*) and stating that it belongs to the Messenger of Allah (peace be upon him and his progeny) and his successors, that is, the Holy Imams (the Prophet's Family (*Ahl al-Bayt*)), Shaykh al-Mufid writes: 'Nobody can do anything with what we enumerated as *anfal* without the permission of the just Imam.[20]

Based on this statement, with regard to what has preceded it and what is said about enjoining the good and prohibiting evil, we can conclude that, like other Shia *ulama*, Shaykh al-Mufid means by 'just Imam' or Imam of integrity' (*al-Imam al-'adil*) someone whose governance is authorised by God, that is, someone who is either immediately appointed by God or is appointed by God's appointees. In contrast to this

---

[20] *Al-Muqna'i*, p. 279.

concept we have the idea of 'usurper Imam [head, leader, ruler], or 'usurper sultan' or 'tyrannical Imam', etc. which signify a ruler whose rule is not vindicated by God and in fact obedience of and allegiance to him is not a religious obligation. It follows that 'just Imam [ruler, sultan]' and like expressions do not meant actual rulers who rule justly, as usurper sultan and like expressions do not refer to rulers who rule tyrannically. The former means a ruler whose rule is endorsed by religion and the latter means one whose rule is not.[21]

A look at other great Shia *faqihs*' views about *wilayat al-faqih* will help clarify the historical background of our discussion.[22]

1- Muhaqqiq al-Hilli (d. 1277)

> It is imperative that 'the tax (portion) of Imam' (*hissat al-Imam*) be apportioned to those who deserve it by the person who has authority because of his deputyship (*niyaba*) by the Imam, as he is also responsible for fulfilling the obligations of the absent (*ghayib*).

Zayn al-Din Ibn 'Ali al-Amili, alias Al-Shahid al-Thani (d.1559), explains:

> By 'the person who has authority because of his delegation by the Imam' is meant the just Shia *faqih* who is fully qualified

---

[21] Of course, one of the prerequisites for such a ruler is justice.

[22] The questions that follow have been compiled and translated into Persian by my friend Muhsin Qumi.

for issuing *fatwa*s. For such a person is the representative and appointee of the Imam [Mahdi].[23]

2- Muhaqqiq al-Karaki (d. 1561)

Shia *faqih*s have consensus on the point that the fully qualified (*jami' al-sharayit*) *faqih,* who is called *mujtahid*, is the deputy (*nayib*) of the Infallible Ones (Peace be upon them) in all the affairs attendant upon the deputyship (*niyaba*). Hence it is obligatory to refer to him in litigation and accept his verdict. If necessary, he can sell the property of the party who refuses to pay what he is due. He has *wilaya* over the absent (*ghuyyab*), children, the fool (*safih*), bankrupts and generally over all that is the fixed responsibility of the ruler appointed by the Holy Imams (Peace be upon them). The report of Omar Ibn al-Hanzala and the like reports evidence this.[24]

Al-Karaki goes on:

If one impartially studies the life and work of the great Shia *ulama* like Sayyid al-Murtaza, Shaykh al-Tusi, Bahr al-'Ulum, and Allama al-Hilli, he finds that this is what they have done and practised, incorporating in their writings what they had believed to be true and authentic.[25]

3- Mawla Ahmad Muqaddas Ardabili (d. 1585)

On the preference of paying *zakat* to the *faqih*, he writes:

---

[23] Zayn al-Din Ibn Ali al-Amili, *Masalik al-Afham*, vol. 1, p. 53.
[24] Muhaqqiq al-Karaki, *Wasai'l al-Muhaqqiq al-Thani*, 'Risala al-Salat al-Juma'', vol. 1, p. 142.
[25] We saw an example of this in remarks made by Sayyid al-Murtaza and Shaykh al-Tusi.

The reason for this, as mentioned before, is that the *faqih* knows best how to spend and apportion it; people from all walks of life refer to him so that he knows who is to be given priority in this matter. The *faqih* is the deputy and successor of the Infallible Ones (Peace be upon them). Hence whatever is given to him is given to the Holy Imams (Peace be upon them).[26]

Hajj Aqa Riza Hamidani (d. 1904) also considers payment (of taxes, etc.) to the *faqih* as payment made to the Twelfth Imam (Peace be upon him): 'For accepting that the *faqih* is the deputy of the Imam (Mahdi) means that payment to him is tantamount to payment made to the Imam (Peace be upon him)'.[27]

4- Jawad Ibn Muhammad Husayni al-'Amili (d.1811)

He is the author of the magisterial *Miftah al-Karama* and is an absolute authority on the views of Shia *faqih*s. He believes that the *faqih* is the deputy and appointee of the Lord of the Age, Imam Mahdi (May God hasten his glad advent):

> The *faqih* is appointed by the Lord of the Age (May God hasten his advent) and this is endorsed by reason, *ijma'*, and reports, *hadiths*.[28] Reason: If the *faqih* was not the representative or deputy of the Lord of the Age, people would be put into a lot of difficulties and their lives would be thrown into disarray. *Ijma'*: After reaching it – as it is said to be the

---

[26] Muqaddas Ardabili, *Majma' al-Fa'ida wa al-Borhan*.

[27] Hajj Aqa Riza Hamidani, *Misbah al-Faqih*, 'Kitab al-Khums', p. 160.

[28] *Ijma'* is the consensus of *ulama* on an issue which demonstrates the existence of a sound proof reflecting the view of the Infallible Ones.

case—we can claim that Shia *ulama* have consensus on this point and their unanimity is authoritative. Traditions: They contain sufficient and convincing evidence for this. An example is the tradition related by Saduq[29] in *Ikmal al-Din* in which the Imam (May God hasten his advent) answering Ishaq Ibn al-Ya'qub's questions writes: 'In contingencies refer to the transmitters (*rawis*) of our traditions (*ahadiths*), for they are my *hujja* (proof, authority) for you and I am God's *hujja*'.[30]

5- Mulla Ahmad Naraqi (d. 1829)

He holds that the *faqih* has *wilaya* (authority) over two sets of things:

First, the *faqih* has *wilaya* over whatever the Prophet and the Imams, rulers over people and the bastions of Islam, have *wilaya* except the cases which, according to *ijma'* or clear statement (*nass*), lie beyond the scope of *wilaya* of the *faqih*.

Second, the *faqih* has *wilaya* over whatever concerns the spiritual and worldly affairs of people which needs to be done because: reason or custom demands it; the livelihood and salvation of some depends on it and it involves the straightening out of the affairs of this and the after-world; divine law has mandated it; *faqihs* have consensus on it; traditions containing the principle of no harm, avoidance of distress and constriction, avoidance of damage to a Muslim, etc. necessitate it; Islam has allowed or disallowed it without assigning any (specific) person or persons to it; or we know that it has to be done and Islam has also allowed it but it is not

---

[29] We will explain the signification of this tradition later.
[30] Husayni al-Amili, *Miftah al-Karama*, 'Kitab al-Qaza', vol. 10, p. 21.

known who is to undertake it. The *faqih* is responsible for all these.

The reason for the first (the *faqih* having *wilaya* over what the Prophet and the Imams have had barring cases where there is evidence for deeming otherwise), in addition to the consensus of *faqih*s, who regard this a truism in Islamic jurisprudence, is the traditions which expressly underscore it.

As to the reason for the second (*wilaya* in affairs which the sacred law of Islam does not allow to be left unattended), there are two proofs besides the consensus of *faqih*s...[31]

6- Mir Fattah Abd al-Fattah (d. 1857-1849)

He argues for *wilayat al-faqih* thus:

First, 'derived consensus'[32] (*ijma' al-muhassal*) is one of the proofs of *wilayat al-faqih*. Some may assume that consensus (*ijma'*) is speculative and non-textual, that is, expressive of an opinion without appearing in textual form, hence it is not to be adduced when there is disagreement on an issue.[33] It is true if by consensus is meant one based on a real law or judgement (*hukm*) in which there is no room for disagreement and exceptions. But a consensus which is based on norm - that is,

---

[31] Ahmad Naraqi, *Awai'd al-Ayyam*, pp. 187-88.

[32] 'Derived consensus' is the unanimity of the views of *ulama* on an issue that is deduced by the *faqih* himself by referring to their *fatwa*s and their works. It stands in contrast to 'reported consensus' where this unanimity of views is only reported by one or a few.

[33] 'Non-textual' proof, in contrast to 'textual proof', is one which is not recorded in textual form. Consensus and the practice of the Prophet and the Imams are non-textual proofs while the Koran and traditions are textual ones.

one achieved to the effect that the *faqih* has *wilaya* in cases where there is no proof of the *wilaya* of someone who is not the ruler – is like consensus on the principle of ritual purity (*tahara*) and hence can be adduced where there is uncertainty. The difference between consensus based on norm and consensus based on actual law or judgement is manifest and the investigation of *faqih*s' works indicates it.

Second, 'reported or transmitted consensus': the works of *faqih*s contain numerous instances of quoting and reporting the consensus on the point that the *faqih* has *wilaya* in all cases where there is no proof of *wilaya* of those who are not *faqih*s.[34]

7- Shaykh Muhammad Hassan Najafi, Author of Jawahir (d. 1849)

On the generality of *wilayat al-faqih* he writes:

The generality of *wilayat al-faqih* is attested to by the practice and *fatwa*s of the experts in jurisprudence (*faqih*). It seems that in their view it is even axiomatic and self-evident.[35]

I believe that God has made obedience of and allegiance to the *faqih*s as 'Holders of Authority' (*uli al-Amr*) incumbent upon us; the proofs of the governance of the *faqih*, especially the tradition by Imam Mahdi[36] (May God hasten his advent), substantiate this.

---

[34] Mir Fattah Maraghi, *Anawin*, p. 354.

[35] Muhammad Hassan Najafi, *Jawahir al-Ahkam*, vol. 16, p. 178.

[36] Shaykh al-Hurr al-Amili, *Wasai'l al-Shi'a*, vol. 18, p. 101 (Kitab al-Qaza, Abwab Sifat al-Qazi, bab: 11-19).

Of course his governance (*wilaya*) extends to everything, (legal or not) involving the religion of Islam and the claim that, on the grounds of 'derived consensus', it is limited to legal provisions and judgements is unacceptable. For *faqih*s have taken the *wilaya* of the *faqih* to be applicable to numerous and different cases and there is no reason not to apply the proofs of governance to these cases. This is confirmed by the fact that Islamic community needs the leadership of the *faqih* more than his authority in religious law.[37]

On the limits of *wilayat al-faqih* he writes:

The words of the Imam [Mahdi] who about the fully qualified *faqih* in non-specific terms says: 'I have appointed him your ruler', as with cases in which he specifically appoints a person: 'I appoint this person your ruler', signify the general, comprehensive governance of the fully qualified *faqih*. Moreover, Imam's statement – 'the transmitters (*rawi*s) of our traditions, are my *hujja* (proof, authority) for you and I am God's *hujja*' – clearly demonstrates the vast powers of the *faqih* such as carrying out Islamic sentences, etc.

Any way, carrying out Islamic sentences and implementing religious injunctions is obligatory at the time of occultation. For being the deputy (*niyaba*) of the Imam (Peace be upon him) in many cases rests with the *faqih*. The *faqih*'s social and political status is the same as the Imam (peace be upon him). There is no difference between him and the Imam (Peace be upon him) in this respect. *Faqih*s and authorities on this issue are unanimous on this point; in their works they frequently underscore the idea of referring to a governor/guardian who is

---

[37] *Jawahir al-Ahkam*, vol. 15, pp. 421-22.

the agent and representative of Imam Mahdi (peace be upon him) at the time of his occultation. If *faqih*s are not to have the general agency and representation (*niyaba*) of the Imam (Peace be upon him), all the affairs of Shias will remain unattended. Those who raise objections about the general *wilaya* of *faqih*, then, seem to be ignorant of jurisprudence (*fiqh)* and the words of the Infallible Ones (Peace be upon them); they have not pondered these words by the Infallible Ones: 'We have designated [the fully qualified] *faqih* our ruler, successor, judge, proof and authority *(hujja)*, ...' Such statements demonstrate that their objective has been the organising and addressing of many of their Shias' affairs, relevant to them, by the *faqih* at the time of occultation. Hence Salar Ibn 'Abd al-'Aziz in his *Marasim* is certain that the Infallible Ones have entrusted *faqih*s with these affairs...

In fine, the issue of the general governance, *wilaya,* of the *faqih* is too axiomatic to argue for.[38]

On the question of authority, *wilaya,* of the *faqih* in legal matters this great jurist writes:

The report (*riwaya*) apparently signifies that the *faqih* is the plenipotentiary agent and representative of the Imam (Peace be upon him). This is the definite meaning of his statement: 'I designate him ruler'. That is, he designates the *faqih* as ruler and authority in legal matters (*qazi*) and other matters relevant to *wilaya*. This is also substantiated by another statement by the Twelfth Imam (Peace be upon him): 'In contingencies refer to the transmitters (*rawi*s) of our traditions [*faqih*s], for they

---

[38] *Ibid.*, vol. 21, pp. 395-97.

are my *hujja* (proof, authority) and I am God's *hujja*'.[39] Here the Imam (Peace be upon him) means that, for you, *faqih*s have authority in all that I have authority, unless something is excepted due to a particular reason. This is not incongruous with the fact that the *faqih* can designate someone who is not a *faqih* as judge in certain legal matters. On the basis of this superintendence and general *wilaya*, the *faqih* (or *mujtahid*) can appoint one of his imitators or followers (*muqallid*) to adjudicate between his followers (*muqallid*s) in accordance with his *fatwa*s which define the lawful (*halal*) and the unlawful (*haram*). The judgement of this person is that of the *faqih* (*mujtahid*), the judgement of the *faqih* is that of the Holy Imams (Peace be upon them) and the judgement of the Imams is that of God... This will prove to be quite clear even certain if we investigate the relevant reports and traditions compiled in *Wasai'l* and other books.[40]

8- Shaykh Murtiza Ansari

Although he does not regard *wilaya* as absolute, he stresses that *wilayat al-faqih* is one of the well-known *fatwi*s of Shia *faqih*s: 'As Jamal al-Muhaqqiqin discussing *khums* has admitted, it is well-known among the Shia that the *faqih* is the agent and representative of the Imam'.[41]

9- Hajj Aqa Riza Hamidani (d. 1904)

In any case, it is evident that the *faqih* of integrity is the deputy of the Lord of the Age in such matters. Shia *faqih*s have

---

[39] See Al-Hurr al-'Amili, *Wasai'l al-Shia'*, vol. 18, p. 101.

[40] *Jawahir al-Ahkam*, vol. 40, p. 18.

[41] Shaykh Murtiza Ansari, *Al-Makasib*, p. 155.

testified to this in their works. Their statements indicate that they regard the deputyship (*niyaba*) of the *faqih* of integrity, authorised by Imam Mahdi (Peace be upon him), in all matters of Islamic jurisprudence as indisputable so much so that some of them have taken consensus to be the pivotal proof of the *faqih*'s general representation (*niyabat al-'ammih*).[42]

10- Sayyid Muhammad Bahr al-'Ulum (d. 1908)

Bahr al-'Ulum discusses the issue of whether or not the proofs of *wilayat al-faqih* demonstrate the generality and all-inclusiveness of *wilaya*:

The important issue here is whether the proofs of *wilaat al-faqih* indicate its all-inclusiveness or not. The answer is: as the Imam (Peace be upon him) is the head of the Muslim community people refer to him in different matters such as issues involving their worldly affairs, their spiritual life and warding off harm and mischief. For every nation has recourse to those in charge in such issues. Evidently, this will help consolidate and fortify the Islamic community that has always been one of Islam's objectives. It follows that to maintain the Islamic community Imam (Peace be upon him) has to appoint a successor and representative who could not be anyone but the fully qualified *faqih*. This is substantiated by traditions such as: 'In contingencies refer to the transmitters of our traditions'. Furthermore, Shia *faqih*s unanimously agree that there are many cases and situations in which people have to refer to the *faqih*. It is notwithstanding the fact that there are no particular reports and traditions regarding these cases. They

---

[42] Hajj Aqa Riza Hamidani, *Misbah al-Faqih*, 'Kitab al-Khums', p. 160-61.

have based their opinion on the generality of *wilayat al-faqih*
on the grounds of reason and traditions; consensus on this
issue is diffused (*mustafaz*).[43] Thanks God the issue is quite
obvious and incontrovertible.[44]

11- Ayatullah Burujirdi (d. 1962)

He regards the governance of the *faqih* in affairs affecting
people as axiomatic and indisputable asserting that the
celebrated and accepted tradition reported by Omar Ibn
Hanzala is not required to prove this:

> ... to conclude, with respect to what followed, no objections
> could be raised about the fact that the just *faqih* is appointed to
> see to the important matters that affect the public. The
> accepted and well-founded tradition reported by Omar Ibn
> Hanzala is not required to prove this though it could be
> adduced as one of the proofs.[45]

12- Ayatullah Shaykh Murtaza Hai`ri

He regards the noble decree (*tuqi'*, seal, signature, decree[46])
of the Hidden Imam (May God hasten his advent) as one of
the proofs of *wilayat al-faqih*:

> The hallowed decree of the Lord of our age (May God hasten
> his advent), which is one of the proofs of *wilayat al-faqih*, is

---

[43] '*Istifaza*' means abundance; a '*mustafiz*', diffused, tradition or
consensus is one which is frequently quoted and reported.

[44] Bahr al-'Ulum, *Balqat al-Faqih*, vol. 3, p. 221 and pp. 232-34.

[45] *Al-Badr al-Zahir*, *Lectures by Ayatullah Burujirdi*, p. 52.

[46] The written and signed reports (*riwayas*) by the Lord of the Age (May
God hasten his advent) passed on to the transmitters of *hadith*s via special
representatives at the time of the minor occultation are called *tu'qi'*.

sufficient evidence of permission for the *faqih* (to set up Friday prayer). We explained the chain of transmission of this decree in *Ibtigha al Fazila*. Some have raised objection to arguing based on this account or report (*riwaya*) asserting that the question asked in it is brief and of limited application. This objection is untenable as the rest of the report has general application and argues for and states a general rule. The brevity here, then, is no problem. Thus, if the question is about some new events and contingencies, the general application of the tradition is not affected. For the rest of the report is inclusive and generalises the reason for issuing the decree. We can roughly argue on the basis of this report thus: 'the *faqih* is the appointed authority, *hujja*, by the Imam. Being the appointed *hujja* by the Imam, commonly, means that the *faqih* has authority in and is to be referred to in whatever concerns the Imam.[47]

13- Imam Khomeini (d. 1989)

Imam Khomeini believes that the *faqih* enjoys absolute (*mutlaqa*) *wilaya*. That is, the fully qualified *faqih* is invested by all the powers and responsibilities of the Twelfth Imam at the time of his occultation unless due to a particular reason certain powers and responsibilities rest with Imam. Thus, he writes:

From what was said we conclude that the Holy Imams (Peace be upon them) have entrusted *faqih*s with whatever over which they have authority, *wilaya*. To except a case from this general rule proof must be adduced that it exclusively rests with Imam (Peace be upon him). Reports (*riwaya*s) such as 'such and such

---

[47] Murtiza Hai'ri, *Salat al-Juma'*, p. 144.

> a thing lies within the powers of the Imam' or 'the Imam has
> commanded so' – and … will not do as the responsibility for
> these affairs, due to the reasons already stated, rests with the
> just *faqih*… We mentioned before that the *faqih* enjoys all the
> powers of the Prophet (Peace be upon him and his progeny)
> and the Twelfth Imam (Peace be upon him) in rule and
> governance.[48]

There are two important points to remember here. First,
some of the aforementioned *faqih*s have stressed that *wilayat
al-faqih* is a social matter on which Shia *faqih*s have
unanimity of opinion. The reason why some of them have
not particularly treated this issue in their works is that taking
it as self-evident they have not felt the need to discuss and
prove it. Furthermore, they have stated the responsibilities
and status of *wilayat al-faqih* throughout their discussion of
different juristic matters and categories so that if these
interspersed legal opinions and judgements were to be
compiled into a single category, it would hardly be less
voluminous than most of the independent categories in *fiqh*.
'The writings of *faqih*s', points out the author of *Jawahir*,
'abound in discussions of referring to *wali al-faqih*; Shia
*faqih*s have frequently stressed the idea of *wilayat al-
faqih*'.[49]

Second, Shia *faqih*s have always taken as incumbent on
them to address and meet the religious and canonical
questions and requirements of people. Accordingly, they
have mostly dealt with more urgent and immediate issues,
with everyday needs of people. Since until before the

---

[48] Imam Khomeini, *Kitab al-Bay'*, vol. 2, pp. 488-89.
[49] *Jawahir al-Ahkam*, vol. 15, p. 422 and vol. 21, p. 395.

formation of Safavid dynasty in Iran issues like governance of the *faqih* had little bearing on Shia communities, *faqih*s took little interest in discussing matters of governance and the duties of the ruler limiting themselves to expressing random views and satisfying the immediate requirements of the believers.[50]

Exceptions in this era, from the minor occultation to the formation of the Safavid dynasty, are only *faqih*s like Sayyid al-Murtaza and philosophers like Khaji Nasir Tusi, the former having a close relationship with Buyid rulers and the latter being the grand vizier of Hulagu Khan for a while, who had to deal with matters of governance and were even to some extent involved in them.

Kashif al-Ghita maintains that these great men associated with the rulers of their time because they believed in the governance of the *faqih* and saw this association as the only way of regaining at least part of the right to govern.[51]

Muhaqqiq al-Karaki is of the same opinion and regards these learned scholars as proponents of governance of the *faqih*.[52]

The establishment of the Safavid rule in Iran changed the situation by forming the first nation-wide Shia government in the country. Although this government was monarchical and the majority of Shia *faqih*s regarded it as usurper, such was the state of the affairs that a number of those *faqih*s saw

---

[50] Such as the remarks of Shaykh al-Mufid which notwithstanding their brevity manifestly indicate the acceptance of *wilayat al-faqih* by that great *faqih*.

[51] *Hashiya-ye Muhaqqiq al-Karaki bar Qawai'd*, MS, p. 36.

[52] *Rasai'l al-Muhaqqiq al-Karaki*, vol. 1, p. 270.

supporting the Safavid kings as the sole way to maintain and strengthen Islam and protect the country from the encroaching of the infidels and foreign powers, hence their close relationship with the monarchy.

Finally, after the formation of the first Islamic government in Iran the late Imam Khomeini, leader of the believers and justice seekers, discussed and shed light on different aspects of governance of *faqih*. We finish this section by quoting this true reviver of Islam in the new age of darkness and ignorance:

> The idea of *wilayat al-faqih* is not an invention of ours. It is a long-standing issue. Mirza Shirazi's *fatwa* on prohibition of tobacco was a mandate for other *faqih*s too as it was a governmental decree... it was not a verdict given, say, about a dispute between a number of people. *Ulama* unanimously supported this *fatwa* of *jihad*, designated defence, because it was a governmental decree. Kashif al-Ghita has elaborated on many of these issues... Among recent *faqih*s, the late Naraqi holds that *faqih*s have the same powers and responsibilities as the Prophet. He also says that it is inferred from the celebrated report of Omar Ibn Hanzala. In any case, this is a long-standing issue on which we just elaborated, discussing different aspects of governance to clarify the issue... It is the self-same issue as conceived of and presented by *faqih*s. We put forward the core of the issue; it is up to the present and future generations to further examine and try to find ways of realising it... [53]

---

[53] Imam Khomeini, *Wilayat al-Faqih*, pp. 172-73.

Governance (*wilaya*) of the Infallible Ones, governance of *faqih*

What followed indicates that in Shia thought accepting the necessity of having someone as the head of the Muslim community it is believed that nobody per se has the right to this except the Almighty God to whose will man's existence and affairs are subject, a fact which binds man to obey Him and comply with His injunctions.[54] It follows that if God enjoins us to obey someone, we must do so; if He stipulates the conditions and qualifications of the ruler leaving the identification of the qualified person to us again we must obey.

Shia has always maintained that God has accorded the Holy Prophet (Peace be upon him and his progeny) and after him the Holy Imams the governance of the Islamic *umma*, a fact substantiated by the four proofs: the Koran, *sunna* (the practice, example and traditions of the Prophet and the Infallible Ones), reason, and consensus.

As for the consensus of the Shia *ulama*, it is so well-known that even the scholars of other Islamic schools do not doubt it. Generally speaking, the principle of '*Imamat*', one of the fundamentals of Shia doctrine, maintains that after the Holy Prophet (Peace be upon him and his progeny) these were the Imams from his Family who were entrusted with the governance of the Islamic *umma*. Hence Shia believes that the Holy Prophet enjoyed the station of '*Imamat*' in addition

---

[54] See Jawadi Amuli, *Wilayat-i-Faqih* (*Rahbari dar Eslam*), p. 29.

to prophethood (*nubuwwa*) and messengership (*risala*).[55]

Prophethood is having knowledge of divine secrets in the world of creation and divine legislation and messengership is the rank enjoyed by those Arch-prophets who are assigned to communicate the divine message and guide people.

As for the intellectual proof, some have adduced the proof of Divine Grace deeming it sufficient to prove that the Prophet or the Imam is the ruler of the Islamic community. A number of *ulama*, however, do not agree that it is sufficient evidence and adduce the proof of Divine wisdom.[56]

The proof of Divine wisdom could be very briefly explained as follows. Proving the existence of God and the afterlife reason concludes that whatever man does has an indelible effect on his life in the hereafter but finds itself unable to discern and probe these effects, their causes and their interactions. Hence the wisdom of God, the creator of the world and man, necessitates showing man the path to salvation through sending messengers. On the other hand, to meet the objective for sending the prophets, i.e. guiding people, they should be infallible and free of all faults in either receiving or communicating divine mandates. Then reason concludes that inerrancy in receiving and

---

[55] By *Imamate* here is meant 'governance and the leadership of the Islamic *umma*'. The other meaning of *Imamate* applied to the Infallible Ones is the possession of divine knowledge that is similar to the status of prophethood. Some have erroneously taken *Imamate* to only mean the latter. See Mahdi Hai'ri Yazdi, *Hikmat va Hukumat*, p. 171.

[56] This stands in sharp contrast to the unfounded view held by some who regard Divine Grace to be the only rational proof here and, unaware of the criticisms, like Fakhr al-Razi's, levelled at it through the centuries, assume to be its first critic. See *Hikmat va Hukumat*, pp. 173-76.

communicating revelation means being free of all faults, even the possibility of inadvertence and forgetfulness is ruled out.[57] The Prophet, then, has to be immune from error in everything. Then reason concludes that Divine wisdom necessitates that the Infallible Ones be in charge of the community. Consequently, Islam definitely assigns the Prophet himself to govern the community. Similarly, pondering the rank of *Imamat* reason finds Imam to be the interpreter of the divine message revealed to the Prophet and arrives at the same conclusion.[58]

In a word, concluding that the Prophet and the Imams are infallible reason sees as the necessary consequence of Divine wisdom investing the governance of the community in them whereby proving them to be holders of *wilaya* in the sense of governance.

There are many Koranic verses proving the *wilaya* of the Holy Prophet.[59] The most manifest of these probably is: 'Nearer of kin unto the faithful is / The Prophet, than they are to their own selves' (Al-Ahzab: 6). This Koranic statement confirms that the Holy Prophet of Islam (Peace be upon him and his progeny) has more authority over the faithful than themselves, that is, his decisions about the private and public affairs of the faithful are prior to those made by themselves and are to be complied with

---

[57] I have discussed this matter in detail in the second volume of *Theological foundations of ijtihad* (Persian).

[58] See *ibid.*

[59] See Muntaziri, *Wilayat al-Faqih*, vol. 1, pp. 37-73.

categorically.[60]

Of course this verse is proof of the absolute *wilaya* of the Holy Prophet (Peace be upon him and his progeny) in the area of the religiously permissible as it is in this area that people are entitled to make decisions for themselves.

According to the widely transmitted traditions and reports the Holy Prophet in the event of the pond (*al-Ghadir*) refers to this Koranic verse where addressing the people he says: 'Am I not nearer unto you than yourselves?' After the people's admission he continues: 'Ali is the *wali* (holder of *wilaya*) of whomever whose *wali* I am'.[61]

Imam Ali (Peace be upon him) and the other Holy Imams (Peace be upon them), then, have the same *wilaya* as that of the Prophet.[62]

Another Koranic verse substantiating the *wilaya* of the Prophet and Imam Ali is: 'Your true *wali* is only Allah, / And His Apostle, and believers, / Those who set up *salat* [prayer] and pay *zakat*, / And who bow down as worshippers' (Al-Ma'ida: 55).

In this Koranic verse, which is the plain proof of Shia belief in *wilaya*, God, respectively, declares His own *wilaya*, that of His Prophet and finally that of those who believe, set up *salat* (regular prayers) and pay *zakat* while bowing in

---

[60] See Sayyid Kazim al-Hai'ri, *Wilayat al-Amr fi 'Asr al-Ghayba*, p. 153 and Muntaziri, *Wilayat al-Faqih*, vol. 1, pp. 37-40.

[61] See Majlisi, *Bahar al-Anwar*, vol. 37, p. 108 and Muntaziri, *Wilayat al-Faqih*, vol. 1, p. 41.

[62] See Sayyid Kazim al-Hai'ri, *Wilayat al-Faqih fi 'Asr al-Ghayba*, p. 153.

worship. This believer according to traditions transmitted by Shias and Sunnis alike is none but Ali Ibn Abi Talib (Peace be upon him).[63]

This verse substantiates the absolute *wilaya* of the Prophet and the Holy Imams (Peace be upon them).

There are also many traditions and reports about this issue a number of which have been already mentioned. An example is the following statement by Imam Sadiq (Peace be upon him) on the above Koranic verse: 'Indeed this verse means that nearer unto and holders of greater authority over you, your affairs, your lives and your properties, till the Day of Judgement, are God, His Prophet and those who believe, that is, Ali and his descendants'.[64]

From the Shia perspective, *wilayat al-faqih* in the age of the occultation is the continuation of the *wilaya* of the Holy Imams (Peace be upon them) which was, in turn, the continuation of the *wilaya* of the Holy Prophet (Peace be upon him). It culminates in the belief that the foremost position in the Muslim community must be held by one who truly knows Islam, that is, the Twelfth Imam in case he is present and *faqih*s in case he is not. This view is based on the fact that the pivotal objective of governance in Islam is to disseminate and establish Divine mandates and values in society the realisation of which demands that the top leader be a person truly cognisant of Islam. Needless to say, this person must also be informed of the world situation and

---

[63] See Al-Suyuti, *Al-Durr al-Manthur*, Al-Bahrani, *Tafsir al-Burhan*, vol. 1, p. 479.

[64] See Shaykh al-Kulayni, *Usul al-Kafi*, vol. 1, p. 288 (Kitab al-Hujja, bab: Ma Nass-Allah wa Rasuluhu 'alal-'Ai'ma, hadith: 3).

competent in running the Islamic society. We will say more on this when we come to the 'requirements of *wali al-faqih*'.

Proofs of *wilayat al-faqih*

There are many ways of substantiating '*wilayat al-faqih*' of which we point out the simplest and most manifest ones.[65]

The point to remember here is that consensus is always regarded as a proof. We have already discussed 'derived' consensus and 'transmitted' one by Shia *ulama* on governance of *faqih*. The consensual proof, however, is acceptable only when those involved base it on some valid evidence solely available to them; as it is, we have access to all their proofs in this issue. Hence, while their unanimous view is a strong indication of the applicability of the proofs, it cannot be treated as an independent argument. Here we limit ourselves to discussing rational and transmitted proofs.

Intellectual proof

We have already pointed out that a society undoubtedly needs a ruler and leader. Matters of governance do not lie outside the sphere of religion. On the contrary, the universal elements of Islam form a perfect system in this area. Far from disallowing the involvement of religion in governmental issue, reason -- on the grounds of Divine wisdom -- stresses its necessity. Thus, if we approach governance from a religious perspective and take its prime task to be maintaining divine values and Islamic teachings, reason demands that the foremost position in such a

---

[65] I have surveyed these ways in detail in my *Al-Hukm al-Eslami fi 'Asr al-Ghayba*.

government be entrusted to someone who is best aware of these issues and is competent as a leader. If the Hidden Imam (Peace be upon him) was present, reason would recognise him as the right person for undertaking this responsibility. In his absence, however, reason assigns the just *faqih*s capable of leadership to this position.

In other words, reason demands that the foremost position in a government based on Islamic beliefs and ideals be held by someone who is well-informed of these beliefs and ideals, that is, by the fully qualified *faqih*.

Transmitted proof

There are many traditions and reports adduced as proofs of *wilayat al-faqih* of which we have here discuss only a few:

1. The report from Imam Ali (Peace be upon him), related by Saduq, in which the Holy Prophet says: "O God! Have mercy on my successors". Asked who his successors were, the Holy Prophet answered: "Those who come after me and transmit my *hadith*s and *Sunna*". There are two essential aspects to be considered in every report (*riwaya*): first, *sanad* (chain of transmission, authority or authenticity); second, signification, since the report under discussion has many *sanad*s and is reported in many books we are certain that it is authentic and verifiable.[66] As to how this report signifies '*wilayat al-*

---

[66] Saduq, *Man la Yahzuruh ul-Faqi*, vol. 4, p. 420 (Bab al-Nawadir, hadith: 5919); Saduq, *Kitab al-Amali*, p. 109 (Majlis: 34, hadith: 4); Saduq, *'Uyun al-Akhbar al-Riza*, vol. 2, p. 37 (hadith: 94); Saduq, *Ma'ani al-Akhbar*, vol. 2, p. 374 (baab: 423); Al-Hurr al-'Amili, *Wasai'l al-Shia'*, vol. 18, pp. 65-66 (Kitab al-Qaza, Abwab Sifat al-Qazi, bab: 8, hadiths: 10, 11, 48, 52); Majlisi, *Bahar al-Anwar*, vol. 20, p. 25 (Kitab al-I'lm,

faqih,' two points are to be noted. First, the Holy Prophet (Peace be upon him and his progeny) had three main responsibilities: disseminating God's message, articulating religious injunctions and guiding people; adjudicating in legal matters and settling disputes; governance and leadership of the Muslim community, that is, *wilaya.* Second, 'those who come after me and transmit my *hadith*s and *sunna*' refers to *faqih*s not transmitters and reporters. For a reporter or transmitter (*rawi*) who solely transmits *hadith*s cannot determine whether what he transmits is genuinely the *hadith* and *sunna* of the Holy Prophet or not. He only narrates what he has heard or seen without having knowledge of its background, its determining principles, its particulars and statements or practices which may contend it and how to account for them. A person who has expertise in such matters and can positively determine if a tradition is that of the Holy Prophet or a certain practice accords with his *sunna* has achieved the status of *faqih*s and is capable of *ijtihad* (independent interpretation or judgement).

Considering these points, this *hadith* signifies that: '*faqih*s are successors of the Holy Prophet' and as the Prophet held many positions and here no specific position has been mentioned it follows that *faqih*s are the Prophet's successors in all these positions.[67]

---

bab: 8, hadith: 83); Hindi, *Kanz al-'Umal*, vol. 10, p. 229 (Kitab al-I'lm min qism al-Aqwal, bab: 3, hadith: 29209).

[67] See Imam Khomeini, *Kitab al-Bay'*, vol. 2, p. 468; Sayyid Kazim Hai'ri, *Asas al-Hukumat al-Eslamiya*, p. 150; Muntaziri, *Wilayat al-Faqih*, vol. 1, p. 463.

Some have raised objection to adducing this report and its like in which the word 'khalifa' (successor) has been used claiming that:

> Khalifa (vicegerent, successor, caliph) has two meanings. First, the literal and original sense that is the sense in which it is used in the Koran. Ex.: 'I / Will place a khalifa on the earth' (Al-Baqara: 30). Or: 'O David! Truly have We made you / A Vicegerent [khalifa] upon the earth,' (Sad: 26).
>
> In the first verse khilifa (vicegerency, succession, caliphate) is a divinely pre-ordained matter not legislated or established; though in the second verse khilifa is a legislated (tashri'i) matter, it only refers to adjudication.
>
> Second, the politico-historical sense that in Islam emerged after the demise of the Holy Prophet. This is a secular concept and phenomenon; something which people rightly or wrongly bestow on an individual hence absolutely different from the high status of Imamat or Prophethood (risala) which are conferred by God.[68]

If we consider the literal meaning of 'khalifa' which is 'succession', we will see that it is always used in the same sense be it in the Koran, traditions and even historical texts; the differences, if any, lie in the mode of 'succession' which is sometimes in divinely preordained positions and sometimes in legislated matters and legal positions. Even in the history of Islam when the term 'khalifa' ('caliph') gained currency after the demise of the Holy Prophet (Peace be upon him and his progeny) it meant that the caliph was the

---

[68] *Hikmat va Hukumat*, pp. 186-87.

successor of the Prophet in governance and administration of the Muslim community. Thus, '*khalifa*' dose not have multiple meanings but a unique one even though the corresponding positions and spheres denoted by this unique meaning may differ.

In the above Koranic verses *khalifa* is also used in the sense of successor and as a specific mode of succession has not been stipulated the application is general signifying that the fully qualified *faqih* is the Holy Prophet's successor in all his positions and responsibilities.

2. The report from the Twelfth Imam (*Tuqi'*) [see n. 46] related by Saduq in his *Kamal al-Din* (*Ikmal al-Din*) from Ishaq Ibn Ya'qub in which the Imam (May God hasten his advent) in answer to one of his questions, personally, writes: 'In contingencies refer to the transmitters (*rawi*s) of our *hadith*s, for they are my *hujja* (authority, proof) for you and I am God's *hujja* (for them)'.[69]

Shaykh al-Tusi relates the same report in *Al-Ghayba* with the difference that it ends with: 'I am God's *hujja* for you' instead of 'I am God's *hujja* for them'.[70]

In Tabarsi's transmission in *Al-Ihtijaj* the report ends only with, 'I am God's *hujja*'.[71]

---

[69] Saduq, *Kamal al-Din* (*Ikmal al-Din*), vol. 2, p. 483 (bab: 45, al-Tuqi'at: al-tuqi' al-rabi').
[70] Shaykh al-Tusi, *Al-Ghayba*, p. 177.
[71] See Shaykh al-Hurr al-'Amili, *Wasai'l al-Shia'*, vol. 18, p. 101 (Kitab al-Qaza, Abwab Sifat al-Qazi, bab: 11, hadith: 9).

Of course, as we will explain, these differences in transmission do not affect the signification of the report.

As regards *sanad* (chain of transmission) it is almost certain that it goes back to Ishaq Ibn Ya'qub: a number of transmitters have reported it from other transmitters who in turn have transmitted it from al-Kulayni from Ishaq Ibn Ya'qub.

No particular attestation of Ishaq Ibn Ya'qub is to be found in books of biography and criticism of traditionists. Some have tried to prove that he is al-Kulayni's brother, though to little avail.[72]

A simpler way is to say that considering the situation of the Lord of the Age (May God hasten his advent) in the era of his minor occultation and the extreme suppression at the time – which had impelled the Imam to go into seclusion and communicate with people only through his chosen representatives – written statements and decrees (*tuqi*'s) would solely be handed to absolutely reliable persons, for they undeniably testified to the fact that the Imam was living and governing. The very fact, then, that the Imam would send an epistle to a person at that time is proof of the reliability of that person.[73]

The question may be raised: How can we be sure that Ishaq Ibn Ya'qub has received this written statement (*tuqi*') and he has not lied about it? The answer is that al-Kulayni who has transmitted this (*tuqi*') from him, considering what followed,

---

[72] Al-Tustari, *Qamus al-Rijal*, vol. 1, p. 786.

[73] I have discussed this as one of the common methods of attestation in *Tahrir al-Maqal fi Kuliyyat al-I'lm al-Rijal*, pp. 109-111.

has definitely been sure of his reliability otherwise he would not report from him. Hence, no room is left for doubt about the reliability and authenticity of this report.[74]

The best way to argue based on this report, as we saw in some of the writings by earlier *faqih*s, is to say that the Imam here puts the two propositions: ' They are my *hujja* for you' and: 'I am God's *hujja*' in a way as to clearly demonstrate that the authority (*hujja*) of the transmitters of the Infallible Ones' *hadith*s – *faqih*s – is identical with the authority of the Imam himself; that is, *faqih*s are the representatives of the Imam among people. Now if we take into consideration the time when this written statement (*tuqi'*) has been issued and take note of the fact that the Imam was preparing Shias for his major occultation and was indeed giving the last counsels, guidelines, and mandates, we will see that it refers to the era of occultation and, as many of Shia *faqih*s have pointed out in the past, designates the fully qualified Shia *faqih* as the successor of the Imam in all affairs including the governance of the Islamic *umma*.

Some have even raised objection to adducing this *hadith* – which is to be found in many texts of *fiqh* of which they only seem to be familiar with Naraqi's *'Awai'd* – and have regarded the recourse to it a result of failure to grasp the meaning of *hujja* due to lack of expertise in philology! They have got themselves into an inextricable tangle by looking for the uses of the word '*hujja*' in logic, philosophy and *fiqh*.[75]

---

[74] Sayyid Kazim Hai'ri, *Wilayat al-Amr fi 'Asr al-Ghayba*, pp. 122-25.

[75] *Hikmat va Hukumat*, pp. 207-14.

'*Hujja*' here means the authority of Master over devoted follower hence the injunctions of the holder of *hujja* have to be complied with. The Imam (Peace be upon him) is God's *hujja* and God will not accept any excuses for disobeying him. The *faqih* is also the Imam's *hujja*, authority and proof, i.e., his demands and directives, be it *fatwa*s and rulings or governmental edicts, are those of the Imam and as such are not to be objected to. Anyway, as we saw time and again in the statements of *faqih*s, there is no doubt that this *hadith*-report refers to *wilayat al-faqih* and the fact that the *faqih* represents the Imam.

Wilayat al-faqih and people

Some have tried to put forward different theses by Islamic *ulama* about the issue of Islamic ruler claiming that 'theory of governance of the *faqih*' is only one of the existing theories in this area which is itself divided in two versions: 'theory of appointment' and 'theory of election'. However, the views of the prominent *faqih*s, in the past and at present, clearly indicate that the only tenable thesis for them has been and is the 'theory of appointment of the *faqih* as *wali* (holder of *wilaya*)'; other theses on this issue have been propounded in the last few decades in the history of Shia thought by those who, usually, are not outstanding figures in the domain of *fiqh*.[76]

The proofs discussed here all indicate the appointment of the *faqih* as *wali* (holder of *wilaya*) which is a proven fact for

---

[76] Of course some recent *faqih*s have postulated theses such as 'election of the *faqih* by people as *wali*', ' supervision of governmental matters by the *faqih*' and '*wilaya* of someone who is not a *faqih* himself but is appointed by the *faqih*'.

well-informed *mujtahids*. Some, however, have deemed as improbable that anyone who achieves *fiqaha* (the station of *faqih*) can have *wilaya* and have construed the apparently 'actual *wilaya*' in related *hadith*-reports as '*wilaya* in station'. In fact, they accept that these *hadith*-reports essentially prove the 'theory of appointment' but as it is something improbable, contrary to their apparent meaning, they should be taken to mean having the station of and being qualified for *wilaya*, that is, *faqih*s are qualified to be in charge of the Islamic community and the one elected by people will have actual *wilaya* or governance.[77]

The question raised concerning this objection is: why is it improbable that *faqih*s be accorded governance? In answer, it has been said that if a number of *faqih*s qualified for having *wilaya* are found at a time, there will be five possibilities as regards the issue of appointment: (1) each one is individually appointed by the Holy Imams (Peace be upon them) to governance and hence can act independently; (2) all are appointed to governance but only one can have actual *wilaya*; (3) only one of them is appointed to governance; (4) all are appointed to governance but everyone's *wilaya* is conditional upon others' consensus; (5) they are appointed to governance as a single body (this possibility is practically the same as (4)).

All of these possibilities are unacceptable. The first possibility results in chaos in society because each *faqih* may have a view inconsistent with others' views on a certain issue. This does not accord with God's wisdom as it undermines the objective of putting in order and

---

[77] Muntaziri, *Wilayat al-Faqih*, vol. 1, pp. 408-09.

administrating the affairs of the Muslim community by forming an Islamic government. In the second possibility there is no way to determine who can have actual *wilaya*. Moreover, the *wilaya* of *faqih*s other than the holder of actual governance would be void and meaningless and hence its establishment would be inconsistent with the wisdom of the All-Wise. By the same token, the third possibility is also disproved. The fourth and fifth possibilities are also ruled out as they are incongruous with common practice. Furthermore, no one has allowed such possibilities.[78]

The above objection has been answered in different ways such as: (1) all *faqih*s are appointed to the governance of the Islamic community hence undertaking this responsibility is a 'general obligation' (*farz al-kifaya*) for them, namely, if someone fulfils this pivotal duty, it would suffice and others will not be responsible any more[79]; (2) the matter of *wilaya* is not like that of congregational prayer in which any one of the just (*'adil*) faithful can become the prayer leader but it is primarily the responsibility of one who is more learned, righteous, courageous and sagacious than others.[80]

Apart from the fact that the first argument is applicable to matters of religious (*shar'i*) obligation rather than legislated ones like *wilaya* it still cannot refute the objection under discussion. For a matter of 'general obligation' is incumbent upon all until someone undertakes it. The same aforementioned five possibilities and objection will remain.

---

[78] *Ibid.*, 409-15.
[79] Jawadi Amuli, *Wilayat-i-Faqih*, p. 186. *Farz al-Kifaya* (general obligation) is something which is obligatory for a group of people until it is fulfilled by one or several of them.
[80] *Ibid.*, p. 187.

The second answer, besides the lack of supporting evidence, would be refuted in case two persons equally share the qualities mentioned; though such parity is extremely rare in reality, from individuals' viewpoint it is quite probable, that is, anyone may think that he is more learned, righteous and courageous than others. Moreover, this answer in a way acknowledges the objection and admits that the most learned, righteous and courageous *faqih* is the one who is entrusted with governance.

This objection is nonetheless refutable. For all *faqih*s accept—and the proofs of *wilayat al-faqih* necessitate—that if *wali al-faqih* (the *faqih* who governs) issues an injunction, it is incumbent upon all, even other *faqih*s bearing *wilaya*, to comply with it. Also, if a *faqih* takes charge of part of the affairs related to *wilaya*, others, even *faqih*s having *wilaya*, are not allowed to interfere.

As such, we take the first of these five possibilities, namely, all *faqih*s of integrity having the station of *wilaya*, to be the case as the assumption of chaos here is ruled out considering that: (1) all even other *faqih*s have to comply with the injunctions of *wali al-faqih*; (2) others, including other *faqih*s, cannot interfere with matters lying within the responsibility of a *faqih*.

Thus, the thesis of the appointment of *faqih* to *wilaya* – which is held by the majority of the great Shia *faqih*s including Imam Khomeini (*quddisa sirruh*) and is consistent with the proofs of *wilayat al-faqih* – is prone to no objections either in theory or in practice. Nonetheless, if the aim is to set a norm not conditioned by a particular time and place, there is no way but to accept election by people.[81]

To elaborate, the designation of all the fully qualified *faqih*s as *wali al-faqih* is consistent with the purport of the proofs supporting it and essentially cannot be objected to and everyone can refer to the *faqih* they recognise as fully qualified in affairs pertaining to *wilaya*.[82] However, if we put this in the broader communal perspective and the administration of society and try to establish laws for it – even on the basis of the well-founded thesis of appointment – we have to ineluctably opt for election. Of course election here is on the basis of 'singling out the fully qualified (*jami' al-sharayit*) *faqih*' not 'singling out *wali* from *faqih*s who are fully qualified' which is the tenor of the 'theory of election'. That is, people elect the fully qualified *faqih* rather than singling *wali* out from those who are fully qualified. That is why indirect election, that is, the election of the experts ('*khubrigan*') by people followed by the election of the fully qualified *faqih* by experts is preferred to direct election, namely, the election of fully qualified *faqih* by people. This issue has been considered in the constitution of the Islamic Republic of Iran hence while it acknowledges the thesis of appointment – as it is manifest both in the negotiations of the experts and the contents of the constitution itself – it prefers the indirect method of electing

---

[81] Thus, the expert representatives in drawing the constitution of the Islamic Republic of Iran, accepting the 'thesis of appointment', ratified popular election. Of course, they preferred indirect election rather than direct one as it better captures the spirit of the thesis of appointment.

[82] As the great Shia *faqih*s have always been people's *marja' al-taqlid*s (sources of emulation) in the past and today.

the leader.[83]

People's role, then, is crucial, even according to the thesis of appointment. Though the governance of the *faqih* owes its legitimacy to Islam and the Holy Imams (Peace be upon them) rather than popular election, the role played by people is not restricted to rendering the government efficient and complying with the commands of the leader. Indeed, it is people's direct or indirect election of 'the fully qualified *faqih*' which determines who is to be the leader.[84]

Governance (*wilaya*) or deputyship (*wikala*) of *faqih*

We demonstrated that the *faqih*, based on the proofs of *wilayat al-faqih*, is in charge of the Islamic community, an office to which he is appointed by the sacred religion of Islam though in the form of a social convention these are people who elect the fully qualified *faqih*.

Also, the proponents of the thesis of election hold that Islam has entitled people to elect one of the fully qualified *faqih*s leader. Thus, they also consider the elected *faqih* to be *wali* and ruler not the deputy or representative (*wakil*) of people in running society.

In contrast to these views, which are held by the absolute

---

[83] Some have wrongly claimed that the idea of election in the constitution of the Islamic Republic of Iran is proof of acknowledging the 'thesis of election'.

[84] Some have tried to substantiate the 'thesis of appointment' and restrict the role of people to that of streamlining the governance by having recourse to certain schools of political philosophy such as Thomas Hobbes's 'theory of obligation'. Such views are not congenial to the tenor of Islamic debates, especially the idea of governance of *faqih*.

majority of Shia *ulama*, some have claimed that as politics or administration of a country are minute, variable and experimental affairs they do not count as immutable divine laws and generally lie beyond the scope of general religious obligations and precepts.[85] Similarly, even the governance of the Infallible Ones sanctioned by Islam is denied and the issue of governance is theorised in a totally different way which in the view of the theoriser [Mahdi Hai'ri Yazdi] is a new approach in the history of political thought.[86] Here we only survey his political view and are not concerned with the assumptions that religion and politics are independent of and unrelated to each other and the Holy Imams (Peace be upon them) are not the leaders and rulers of society—views which run counter to the spirit of being religious, the latter certainly contradicting the fundamentals of Shia creed.

The theory of 'joint ownership', postulated as the basis of this putatively new political philosophy, shorn of the bombastic phraseology of the theoriser [Hai'ri Yazdi], can be summarised as follows.

As man possesses volition, all his actions are merely natural phenomena. By dint of his dynamic, adaptive nature he chooses a place where he can live freely; this culminates in a natural, exclusive relationship between him and the place he has chosen as his habitat which is called 'private ownership'. This ownership is exclusive by virtue of living in a private space and shared-private by virtue of living in the larger shared-private space. These two kinds of ownership are both natural, as they are conditioned by nature, and private, as

---

[85] *Hikmat va Hukumat*, pp. 64-65.
[86] *Ibid.*, pp. 171-72.

each individual independently enjoys them. Individuals who out of this natural necessity choose contiguous habitats enjoy these two kinds of private ownership: exclusive and shared. They all enjoy the personal, exclusive ownership of the small space of 'home' and' the joint ownership of the larger space of surrounding 'environment'. Practical reason impels these individuals, who are the joint owners of their country, to deputise a person or a group of persons who will dedicate themselves to ensuring the peaceful co-existence of the inhabitants. If these individuals are not unanimous as whom to deputise, the only way out will be acting according to the view of the majority. This is analogous to the case where some persons have inherited a property as joint owners and have not yet divided it. Here the only way for the inheritors to exert individual or joint ownership is to mandate someone to maintain and protect against unwarranted claimants the property on their behalf; if it happens that they are not all ready to accept this mandate, the only way out will be to yield to the vote of the majority.[87] The claims made here are: (1) man's ownership of his private habitat is a personal, exclusive, natural affair rather than a contractual one; (2) individuals enjoy joint ownership of the larger habitat, shared environment, naturally rather than contractually; (3) governance of a land means that a person or a group of person have been deputised by the joint owners to bring about an ideal living condition; (4) in case all the joint owners do not agree on an agent or deputy, the view of the majority will have priority.

The first claim – originating in a legal debate and marshalled, with a touch of philosophy, as a new thesis – is

---

[87] *Ibid.*, pp. 100-07.

only applicable to a piece of land not owned by anybody that someone occupies and cultivates.[88]

The second claim neither can be substantiated nor has a clear meaning, for it raises the question: Where is the limit of the larger habitat or shared environment of an individual? Is it just his quarter? Or is it a village or town or even a country or the world?

'According to the thesis of joint ownership', writes the theoriser probably in answer to the above questions, 'a country is a large free space chosen out of necessity by a number of people as their jointly owned habitat'.[89]

This does not help clarify things as it does not tell us why, for instance, the Iranian villagers living near the Iraqi boundary are not the joint owners of part or the whole of Iraqi territories while they are the joint owners of territories lying much further away in Iran.

The implication of the third claim, regarding the ruler as the agent or deputy of the joint owners of a country, is that, as the theoriser [Yazdi] also admits, the owners can depose the ruler at any time since contractual power of attorney is revocable by the client at any time.[90]

Such a rule, from the viewpoint of political philosophy, can have no power base. For here the ruler is the agent or deputy of people and the deputy cannot oblige or compel his client

---

[88] This is stated in a *hadith*-report as: 'Whoever cultivated a piece of land owns it'. See Majlisi, *Bahar al-Anwar*, vol. 76, p. 111 (hadith: 10).

[89] *Hikmat va Hukumat*, p. 113.

[90] *Ibid.*, p. 120.

to do something even if it is particularly related to his power of attorney. For instance, if someone gives power of attorney to a person to sell his house at a fixed price, the agent cannot compel his client to sell the house at that fixed price though he can personally do it as long as his power of attorney remains in force. This view, then, cannot be an acceptable political thesis as it dose not have a clear, reasonable idea of power.

The fourth claim contradicts the very thesis of joint ownership. For something which is jointly owned can be interfered with only if each and every one of the owners agree to it and there is no reason why the majority rule should be accepted. Hence, if all the heirs in the above example do not agree to the agency of a certain person, he cannot interfere with the jointly owned property on the basis of the agreement arrived at by the majority. Thus, the idea that there is no way but to accept the majority rule in reality disproves the thesis under discussion rather than proving it.

On the other hand, even if there is a consensus by all the joint owners of a country, each and every one of them can revoke the power of attorney and depose the ruler. Can such a thesis be acceptable in political thought?

There is no need to argue for the well-grounded thesis of 'wilayat al-faqih' or argue against the baseless theory of 'deputyship', though some have done so.[91]

Qualifications of *wali al-faqih*

As argued before, only someone who has achieved *fiqaha*

---

[91] Jawadi Amuli, *Wilayat al-Faqih*, pp. 110-12.

(station of *faqih*) and is capable of deriving divine laws from reliable sources can be in charge of the Islamic community. Of course the *hadith*-reports specify this person as 'transmitter of *hadith*s or *sunna* of the Holy Imams' and only a *faqih* or *mujtahid* can identify the sayings and doings which are truly those of the Infallible Ones (Peace be upon them). Probably one reason for the use of the expression 'transmitters of the *hadith*s and *sunna*' of the Holy Imams is that the terms '*faqih*' and '*mujtahid*' may not have had their modern meanings at that time; or it may be that the *faqih*s of that time have also been transmitters of *hadith*s though not all the transmitters have been *faqih*s.

In any case, as a prerequisite, the ruler of the Muslim community is to have achieved *fiqaha*, that is, 'absolute *ijtihaad*'; namely, he has to be able to make the right decisions and judgements on the basis of the religious sources. Moreover, this *ijtihad*, the ability to make independent judgements and interpretations, should not be limited to a particular field ('partial *ijtihad*').[92]

The other prerequisite for the head of the Muslim community is 'justice'. Though this has not been stipulated in the transmitted proofs of *wilayat al-faqih*, reason demands that a community founded on an idea cannot be run by someone who does not believe in that idea.[93] Besides, there are Koranic verses and *hadith*-reports which ban obedience of the unjust and the corrupt such as: 'Nor follow those whose hearts We have allowed / To be of Our remembrance,

---

[92] *Ibid.*, pp. 121-22; Sayyid Kazim Hai'ri, *Asas al-Hukumat al-Eslamiya*, p. 247.

[93] Muntaziri, *Wilayat al-Faqih*, vol. 1, pp. 289-300.

heedless, / Pursuing only their own whims, whose business, / In Life, is nothing but excess!' (Al-Kahf: 28).

Us-l al-Kafi contains a report from Imam Baqir (Peace be upon him) in which the Holy Prophet (Peace be upon him and his progeny) is reported to have said: '*Imamat* and governance befits only a man who has three traits: (1) piety which makes him eschew sin; (2) forbearance whereby he bridles his wrath; (3) benignity in rule rendering him a kind father unto those he rules over'.[94] This report also points out another requirement, that is, only the just *faqih* who has the ability to cope with the responsibility of administrating the Islamic community can become the ruler. This is what common sense demands too.

Thus, the fundamental qualifications of the Islamic ruler are: *fiqaha* (having the station of *faqih*), justice ('*idala*), and the ability to administrate the Islamic community.

The limits of wilayat al-faqih

The proofs of '*wilayat al-faqih*' demonstrate that the *faqih* is the ruler of the Islamic community at the time of occultation (*ghayba*). Hence the *faqih* has all the responsibilities and powers which reason demands the leader of society have. This is a point particularly driven home by the transmitted proofs, especially the noble *tuqi*' of the Hidden Imam (May God hasten his advent). *Wilaya* in this sense is called 'absolute *wilayat al-faqih*' in contrast to 'limited *wilayat al-faqih*'. This absoluteness' is in two areas: (1) people over whom the *faqih* has *wilaya* (*mawla 'alayhim*); (2) affairs in

---

[94] Al-Kulayni, *Al-Kafi*, vol. 1, p. 407 (Kitab al-Hujja, bab: Ma Yajib min Haqq al-Imam 'alal-Ra'ya, hadith: 8).

which he has authority.

As to (1), the *faqih* has *wilaya*, authority, over each and every member of the Islamic community, Muslims and non-Muslims, *mujtahid* and lay, his imitators (*muqallid*s), etc., even himself. As this is indicated, as already mentioned, by the transmitted proofs. Moreover, reason demands that the leader of society have such authority.

In contrast, some have considered one of the senses of the word '*wilaya*' in which '*mawla 'alayh*' (one who is subject to *wilaya* or guardianship) is incapable of discharging his own affairs and recognising what is in or against his interests deeming that '*wilayat al-faqih*' is only applicable to this particular area, that is, '*qussar*' (the incapable ones: the minor, the fool, the absent). However, as mentioned before, '*wilaya*' is used in two senses in Islamic law: one related to the *qussar*; the other which is used in *wilayat al-faqih* has nothing to do with the concept of *qussar*.

'*Wilayat al-faqih*', then, does not mean that '*mawla 'alayhim*' (those subject to *wilaya*) are *qussar*. The claim that "'Islamic republic governed by *wali al-faqih*" is oxymoronic', then, is unfounded as *wilaya* here does not mean that '*mawla 'alayhim*' (those subject to *wilaya*) are incapable.[95] While admitting the capability of those subject to it, *wilaya* still rests as it is impossible to administer the community without it. This is the reason why even other *faqih*s — according to the well-known and correct thesis of appointment — are obliged to obey the *faqih* who has undertaken the governance of the Muslim community; how

---

[95] *Hikmat va Hukumat*, p. 216.

could the proofs of *wilayat al-faqih* apply to them if their allegiance to *wali al-faqih* was due to their incapability?

Regarding item (2), the *faqih* has authority in all the affairs of the community and can issue edicts and rulings about them the compliance with which will be obligatory on all. Transmitted proofs and the requirements of leadership bear this out.

Of course since it is Islam which has authorised the governance of *faqih*, it follows that he has to act within the limits set by it. If what he intends to exert his authority about lies within religiously permissible (*mubah*), that is, neither obligatory (*wajib*) nor prohibited (*haram*) though possibly recommended (*mustahab*) or undesirable (*makruh*), then the criterion for the exertion of authority (*wilaya*) will be 'expediency'. Namely, if the banning or enjoining of something is in the interest of the public or the Islamic government or a group of people, the *faqih* can act accordingly, very much like the case with private life where people can do whatever they deem is in their interest provided it is religiously permissible. This is best evidenced by the Koranic verse: 'Nearer of kin unto the faithful is/ the Prophet, than they are to their own selves,' (Al-Ahzab: 6). The verse also proves the governance of *faqih*. The Prophet (Peace be upon him and his progeny), the verse indicates, has a greater claim to the faithful than they have to themselves so he is fitter to command or forbid them to do something. So is it with *wali al-faqih* who, according to the proofs of *wilayat al-faqih*, has the same powers and responsibilities as the Prophet in leading the Islamic community.

The *faqih*'s exertion of authority in matters about which

there is a binding commandment in *sharia* – obligatory or forbidden matters – in a way as to be at variance with or declare as unnecessary the binding nature of the commandment is conditional on being attentive to the possibility of 'mutual exclusion' (*tazahum*). 'Mutual exclusion' is the case where it is impossible to simultaneously comply with and implement two religious obligations as obeying one results in disobeying the other. Here the more important obligation is to be given priority over the other one, which is also important in its own right.

Recognising such priorities in private life is upon the individual themselves but in public life making decisions is such matters – which are binding for all – rests with the head of the community.

Furthermore, it is the duty of the *faqih* to implement Islam's blueprints in different areas of man's social life, which again restricts his authority.

Absolute *wilayat al-faqih* and totalitarian rule

It should be clear by now that there are restrictions on *wali al-faqih*'s powers as in exerting them he has to take into consideration factors such as expediency, mutual exclusion and the priority of implementing Islamic blueprints in different spheres. In our discussion in chapter I we saw that it is imperative that the *faqih* take advantage of the expertise of the experts in different fields of human sciences as it is the prerequisite for deriving the appropriate mechanism in every area.

The 'absolute *wilayat al-faqih*', then, is a technical juristic (*fiqhi*) term referring to the scope of *wilaya* and those subject to it (*mawla 'alayhim*); it does not mean at all that there are no restrictions and limits on the exertion of the powers and authority of *wali al-faqih* (no *faqih* has ever held such a view which is not even acceptable about the Holy Imams). We believe that even God rules according to some criteria. How is it possible, then, that the *faqih* wilfully rule over everyone and in every area unlimited by any criteria?

Unfortunately, ignorance or feigning ignorance about this issue has caused some to identify 'absolute *wilaya*' with 'totalitarian rule'. However, in 'totalitarian' rule there are no restrictions on the power of the ruler and he does not feel obliged to comply with any laws or criteria. As we saw, form the viewpoint of the believers in God's justice, such a thing is not acceptable even about the Infallible Ones and God Himself.

The constitution and absolute *wilayat al-faqih*

As we saw, the proofs of *wilayat al-faqih* prove absolute *wilaya* for the fully qualified *faqih*. Supposing a government with *faqih* at its head is formed in a country and, under the guidance of the said *faqih*, a constitution is legislated in which the limits of the direct interference of the *faqih* are specified leaving the charge of other governmental areas to other statesmen while acknowledging the supremacy of *wali al-faqih*, a number of questions are raised. First, can the said *faqih* directly interfere in areas beyond the scope specified in the constitution? Second, can he change the constitution itself? Third, what is the status of this constitution in *wilayat al-faqih* scheme of government, especially regarding the thesis of appointment?[96]

We have already pointed out that when the *faqih* issues a decree in accordance with *sharia* and what circumstances demand, it is obligatory on all including himself to comply with it. The constitution is in fact a set of laws legislated in accordance with divine precepts to meet the demands of particular circumstances hence while these demands stand no one, not even the jurist leader, can breach them.

Thus, while the constitution remains in force, on account of standing demands giving rise to it, the *faqih* must act within its perimeters. Of course if, as discerned by the *faqih* or his expert advisors, these demands change necessitating new laws, the *faqih* can order the constitution to be replaced or modified. This answers the first two questions. As to the third question, it should be noted that when an Islamic government is formed in a country in which the fully qualified *faqih* is the leader there will always be people who, either on the basis of their independent judgement or as a result of the view of another *faqih*, do not accept the governance of *wali al-faqih* or do not agree on the scope of his powers. This minority do not see submitting to all or some of these powers as binding but regard all the citizens of the country to be bound over by a sort of 'national covenant'. The constitution, which is ratified by the public in a referendum, is an example of such a 'national covenant'.

The concept of country and territory in Islam

In contemporary political geography, the world is divided

---

[96] These questions were actually raised about the constitution of the Islamic Republic of Iran resulting in extensive debates.

into countries with conventional and internationally recognised boundaries run by their respective governments. According to certain criteria those who live in a country are regarded as its 'citizens' and others as 'foreigners'. Some of the laws of a country apply to the citizens, some apply to the resident foreigners and some apply to both.

Does Islam acknowledge such geographical boundaries? In other words, what is Islam's conception of the world?

The answer to the above question is that Islam regards itself to be the religion for all the world at all times. Territories where the majority of people submit to this divine creed is deemed 'the abode of Islam' (dar al-Islam) and the rest of the world is deemed 'territory of unbelief' (dar al-kufr). The only boundaries acknowledged in Islam, then, are those of faith and the true faith, from the Islamic point of view, is Islam itself: 'Religion in the sight of God,/Is certainly Islam' (Ali-'Imran: 19).

The realm of Islam, then, is a uniform one and conventional boundaries do not affect its monolithic nature. Ideally, this uniform realm should be ruled by one of the Infallible Ones and the world government of the Awaited Imam (Mahdi) will realise this ideal. In the era of occultation (ghayiba) if circumstances allow and it is deemed expedient that Muslim territories be administrated as a uniform realm, the fully qualified faqih is to take charge of this uniform realm. However, it may be deemed expedient that each Muslim territory be administrated by a faqih, especially one who is a native of that land. Thus, as a principle in the political doctrine of Islam, the realm of Islam is uniform but depending on the advisable political mechanism it can be divided into and run as smaller unites such as countries or provinces.

Wilaya and *marja'iyya* (religious authority)

We mentioned that the Holy Prophet of Islam (Peace be upon him and his progeny) had three main stations: (1) communicating God's message, articulating religious precept and guiding people; (2) arbitration and settling of disputes; (3) governance and administration of the Islamic community. We also saw that all these stations and responsibilities rest with *faqih*s of integrity in the era of occultation.

In Shia thought, *marja'iyya* has been a combination of giving *fatwa*s or decrees (*ifta*) and '*wilaya*' so that grand *marja'*s (religious authorities) would be both people's guides in core commandments of *sharia* and their leaders in particular social issues.

Distinguishing between *ifta* and *wilaya* and taking only the former to be the responsibility of *marja'iyya* raises a number of questions. First, is it right to dissociate *marja'iyya* from leadership so that someone be people's *marja'* (authority to be referred to) in religious commandments and someone else be the leader of the Islamic community? Second, supposing this dissociation is possible and permissible, is it right to have a multiplicity of leaders and *marja'*s or should there be only one leader and one *marja'*? Or does one admit multiplicity and the other does not? Third, supposing leadership is dissociable from *marja'iyya*, are *marja'*s to be referred to for decrees or *fatwa*s in all social and individual issues?

Here we have to distinguish between '*fatwa*' issued by

marja's and '*hukm*' (order, command) issued by the leader. *Fatwa* is the kind of decree which a *mujtahid* deduces from religious sources in an attempt to find the core divine commandment concerning an issue to be followed by his *muqallid*s (imitators, followers). Thus, *fatwa* is the deduction of universal religious (*shar'i*) precepts in a particular area from religious sources employing known and accepted methods of interpretation and reasoning in *ijtihad.*[97]

The leader, however, with regard to the core divine commandments, Islamic blueprints and the circumstances attendant on a particular issue assigns all, a group or a certain person a duty. This is called *hukm*. '*Hukm*', then, pays heed both to the fundamental divine commandments and the universal, eternal Islamic values and ideals as well as the demands of particular situations; hence it remains in force as long as these demands have not changed.

Of course, as with the *hukm*s (order) of the leader (*wali al-faqih*), *sharia* regards compliance with the *fatwa*s of *faqih*s of integrity obligatory and legitimate with the difference that the *fatwa* of a *faqih* is binding on himself and his imitators (*muqallid*s) whereas all have to comply with the *hukm* of the leader.[98]

---

[97] Imam Khomeini (*qudissa sirruh*) has called these methods '*ijtihad-i Jawahiri*' (*ijtihad* as practiced in *Jawahir*) or 'traditional *fiqh*'.

[98] Thus, at times religious precepts are divided in two categories: (1) divine commandments; (2) *wilai* (pertaining to *wilaya*) injunctions, the former referring to the permanent, core commandments (*fatwa*s) and the latter to the injunctions (*hukm*s) of the leader.

Dissociation of *marja'iyya* from leadership

Now let us turn to the first question. We saw that the *faqih* of integrity takes charge of the leadership of the Islamic community. But *marja'iyya* in the sense of issuing *fatwa*s is a different matter. The concept of *marja'iyya* presupposes *taqlid* (imitation or emulation), that is, a *marja'* has a number of *muqallid*s (imitators or followers).

Taqlid has the negative overtone of blind imitation in Persian. The saying '*taqlid* (imitation) is the bane of man's life' intimates such negative connotations. As a term in *fiqh*, however, *taqlid* denotes the referring of a lay person to an expert in an issue which requires expertise. As such it is something quite reasonable and commonsensical. Apart from this rational argument, there are also textual proofs of *taqlid* such as the Koranic verse: 'so, if you lack the knowledge, /Ask the People of Invocation' (Al-Nahl: 43).

Thus, the reason for a *faqih* being a *marja'* (source to be referred to) is his expertise in *fiqh* and his ability to deduce divine precepts from religious sources whereas what licenses a *faqih*'s leadership, besides this, is his ability to administrate the Islamic community in accordance with the Islamic values and criteria. Hence, it is possible that of two *faqih*s one be preferable for *marja'iyya* due to his greater knowledge in *fiqh* and the other be preferable for leadership due to his greater capability in running the community.[99]

---

[99] This is called the 'prerequisite of *'A'lamiyyat* (being the most learned); referring to 'the most learned' *marja'* is obligatory where: (1) the decrees of 'the most learned' (*'a'lam*) and the non-*'a'lam* differ; (2) there exists a big gap between in terms of knowledge between the most learned *marja'* and other *marja'*s so that, in the specialists' opinion, the latter's decrees

Hence, dissociation of *marja'iyya* from leadership is something reasonable and at times necessary.

Multiplicity in leadership, multiplicity in *marja'iyya*

As to the second question, multiplicity or uniformity in leadership and *marja'iyya*, it has to be noted that as referring to a *marja'* is the referring of the unknowing to the knowledgeable, or the layman to the expert, it is possible but desirable to have numerous *marja'*s in the community. However, there has to be only one leader as the leadership and governance of the Islamic community demands that there exist only one source of decision-making so as to avoid chaos and disturbance. Having just one leader is especially important for in Islam the 'abode of Islam' is in reality indivisible; however, it is possible to have regional or other forms of leadership as circumstances may demand in which case the leaders have to be in harmony so as to avoid division in the Islamic *umma*. In contrast, in issuing decrees (*fatwas*) it is not necessary that all *marja'*s have similar *fatwas* concerning an issue but it is incumbent on each *faqih* to give the *fatwa* which to his knowledge is the right one.

The rule, then, is to have a single leader and numerous *marja'*s though it could be the other way round too. It is also possible to have only one leader and one *marja'* or even one leader who is also the *marja'*.

(*fatwas*), though of expert value compared with the layman's opinion, lack expert value compared with the former's.

The limits of following (*taqlid*) *marja*'s other than the leader

As to the third question, the possibility of following (*taqlid*) the non-leader in all issues, once again we have to point out that when the leader issues a *hukm* (command, order) regarding a matter, he considers *sharia* and the relevant Islamic blueprints besides the demands of the circumstance having as his criterion his own *fatwa* regarding that matter. We also pointed out that all are duty-bound to follow the command of the leader. Now, if people can follow (*taqlid*) the opinion of *marja*'s other than the leader in all individual and social issues while being obliged to comply with the commands (*hukm*s) of the leader, they may face some difficulties. Namely, it may so happen that the leader give a command (*hukm*) on the basis of his own *fatwa* concerning a particular public issue admitting that had his *fatwa* been different, he would not have given this command. What happens to people's obligation to comply with the commands of the leader if it so happens that this 'different' *fatwa* be actually that of the *marja*' or *marja*'s followed (*taqlid*) by them?

With regard to this problem it seems that as compliance with the commands of the leader is obligatory on everyone, even *fuqaha*s, people cannot follow (*taqlid*) the opinion of *marja*'s other than the leader in social matters.

Conclusion

We tried to shed some light on the most important aspects of the governance of *faqih*. The issue of *wilayat al-faqih* is one of the cornerstones of the political doctrine of Islam which is itself part of the Islamic political system. The full discussion of these issues lies far beyond the scope of this brief survey.

Bibliography

The Holy Koran

Nahj-ul-Balagha

Al-Bahrani, Sayyid Hashim al-Husayni. 1375/1955, *Tafsir al-Burhan*, Qum.

Al-Firuz Abadi, 1407/1987, *Al-Qam-s al-Muhit*, Beirut.

Al-Hindi, 'Alai'ddin, 'Ali al-Muttaqi Ibn Hissam al-Din. 1405/1985, *Kanz al-'Ammal fi Sunan al-Aqwal wa al-A'fal*, Beirut.

Al-Hurr, al-'Amili. 1401/1981, *Wasai'l al-Shia'*, Tehran.

Al-Husayni al-'Amili, Sayyid Muhammad Jawad. *Miftah al-Karama fi Sharh Qawaid al-'Allama*, Qum, n.d.

Al-Juhari, Esma'il Ibn Hamad. 1407/1987, *Al-Sahah Taj al-Lugha wa Sahah al-'Arabiyya*, n.p.

Al-Karaki, 'Ali Ibn al-Husayn. *Rasai'l al-Muhaqqiq al-Thani*, n.p., n.d

.... *Hashiyi-ye Muhaqqiq-i Karaki bar Qawai'd*, MS.

Al-Kulayni, Muhammad Ibn Ya'qub. 1401/1981, *Al-Kafi*, Beirut.

Al-Majlisi, 1403/1983, *Bahar al-Anwar*, Beirut.

Al-Mufid, Abu 'Abdallah Muhammad Ibn Muhammad. 1410/1989, *Al-Muqna'i*, Qum.

Al-Qayumi, 1347/1928, *Al-Misbah al-Munir*, n.p.

Al-Suyuti, 1314/1896, *Al-Durr al-Manthur*, Cairo.

Al-Tusi, Shaykh Muhammad Ibn Muhammd. *Al-Ghayba*, n.p., n.d.

Al-Tusturi, Muhammad Taqqi. 1410/1989, *Qamus al-Rijal*, Qum.

Al-Zubaydi, Murtaza. *Taj al-'Arus min Jawahir al-Qam-s*, Beirut, n.d.

Ansari, Shaykh A'zam Murtaza. 1375/1955, *Al-Makasib*, Tabriz,.

Ardabili, Al-Mawla Ahmad al-Muqaddas. 1406 / 1986, *Majma' al-fai'da wa al-Burhan fi Sharh Irshad al-'Azhan*, Qum.

Bahr al-'Ulum, Sayyid Muhammad. 1402/1982, *Balghat al-Faqih*, Tehran.

Hadwi Tehrani, Mahdi. 1992, *Tahrir al-Maqal fi Kulliyyat I'lm al-Rijal*, Tehran.

Hai'ri Yazdi, Mahdi. 1995, *Hikmat va Hukumat*, n.p.

Hai'ri, Sayyid Kazim. 1414/1993, *wilayat al-Amr fi 'Asr al-Ghayba*, Qum.

.... *Asas al-Hukumat al-Eslamiya*.

Hai'ri, Shaykh Murtaza. *Salat al-Juma'*, n.p., n.d.

Hamidani, Hajj Aqa Riza. *Misbah al-Faqih*, n.p., n.d.

Ibn Faris, Abul Husayn Ahmad. *Mu'jam Maqai's al-Lugha*, Qum, n.d.

Imam Khomeini, *Kitab al-Bay'*, Qum, n.d.

Jawadi Amuli, 'Abdullah. 1407/1987, *Wilayat-i- Faqih (Rahbari dar Eslam)*, Tehran.

Maraghi, Mir Fattah. *Al-'Anawin*, n.p., n.d.

Mui'n, Muhammad. 1360/1941, *Farhang-i Farsi*, Tehran.

Muntaziri, Husayn 'Ali. 1408/1987, *Dirasat fi Wilayat al-Faqih wa Fiqh al-Dawlat al-Eslamiya*, Qum.

Najafi, Muhammad Hassan. 1981, *Jawahir al-Ahkam fi Sharh Sharayii' al-Eslam*, Beirut.

Naraqi, Mawla Ahmad. 1408/1987, *'Awai'd al-Ayyam*, Qum.

Nuri, Mirza Husayn. *Mustadrak al-Wasai'l*, Qum, n.d.

Sadr, Sayyid Muhammad Baqir. 1402/1982, *Eqtisaduna*, Beirut.

Saduq, Muhammad Ibn 'Ali Ibn al-Husayn. 1390/1970, *Man la Yahzaruh al-Faqih*, Tehran.

.... *Al-Amali*, n.p., n.d.

....   1399/1979,
Ma'ani al-Akhbar, Beirut.

.... *Kamal al-Din wa
Tamam al-Ni'mat*, n.p., n.d.

.... *'Uyun   al-Akhbar
al-Riza*, n.p., n.d.

Zayn al-Din, al-Jabal al-'Amili (al-Shahid al-Thani).
Masalik al-Afham fi Sharh Sharayi' Al-Eslam, Qum, n.d.